Jane's Patisserie

EASY FAVOURITES

Jane's Patisserie

EASY FAVOURITES

SIMPLE SWEETS & STRESS-FREE TREATS

JANE DUNN

EBURY PRESS

Contents

Introduction

Hey! I'm Jane and I'd like to welcome you to my new book. I'm a blogger, baker, food-obsessed author and this is my fourth book, filled with even more delicious recipes that I just know you're going to love!

For the readers who are new here, ten years ago I decided to go to cookery school and really push my passion for food into something that I could do every day. I wanted to learn about all things food; where it comes from, what you can do with it, flavour profiles and basically how to make something delicious as easily as possible.

My blog, *Jane's Patisserie*, was a hobby that I started as a way to continue my learnings from cookery school and I had no idea that it would develop into the amazing, life-changing business that it is today. I have been blogging for over nine years now and my job evolves constantly – so I never get bored!

I went from taking over my parents' kitchen, to moving into my very own studio so that I could focus on developing the best recipes to share with my followers and at-home bakers too. Cooking on stage for thousands of people and on live TV, reaching new audiences, is something that the younger me could never have dreamed of. I'm so grateful that it's been part of my journey, and what an amazing journey it's been. I can't thank my followers enough – without you none of this would have happened!

After my first three books were such successes, I wanted to go back to basics and think about what it is that people come to my recipes for. This book, *Jane's Patisserie Easy Favourites*, is exactly that! We are all busy, with so much going on day-to-day that we don't have much time on our hands, but we all want reliable recipes for tasty and delicious food that is easy to make, and so SO good.

My recipes have always been about levelling up your baking in simple ways for the biggest impact, and that always starts with an easy recipe. This book is packed with easy-to-follow ideas for instant favourites. With shorter methods covering basic skills and all my best hints and tips, this book will bring new levels of deliciousness to your kitchen and to your baking expertise.

As well as being split into chapters for all of your favourite types of bakes – from **Cakes, Cupcakes & Muffins, Cookies & Traybakes** to **Savoury Meals** – I have also included tags for recipes that require less time (30 minutes or less), just a handful of ingredients (five ingredients), simple dishes that cook all-in-one tin, pan or pot (One-Pan), recipes that require no baking time at all (No-Bake) and more!

As always, this book contains a handful of delicious existing blog favourites that you guys make over and over and over – hello **Speculoos Blondies** (page 91) and my viral classic **School Cake** (page 46) – as well as 70 brand new and exclusive recipes. I can't wait for you to try my deliciously chewy and chocolatey **Crinkle Cookies** (page 72), the zingy **Raspberry Crumble Bars** (page 98), or for those who fancy a savoury treat my simple **Frying Pan Pizzas** (page 226) and gooey **Cheesy Ham and Leek Bake** (page 194) are perfect for cosy weeknight dinners too. I want people to turn every page and make an audible hunger sound, to fold corners or stick a Post-it note on every recipe they want to make – as that's what I do too!

I hope that these recipes become your go-tos, to make cooking easier any day of the week, to cook for yourself or for a crowd, for a rainy Sunday, a birthday or any occasion you need. I hope you all love the dishes in this book as much as I do.

Jane x

EASY FAVOURITES

CAKES, CUPCAKES & MUFFINS

We all know that we need a decent amount of sweet cakey bakes, right? This section features some delicious blog favourites, including a Lemon Drizzle Traybake (page 44) and School Cake (page 46), alongside my Brownie Loaf Cake (page 38), Tiramisu Cupcakes (page 56) and a Sticky Ginger Loaf Cake (page 40).

COOKIES & TRAYBAKES

I would happily bake and enjoy a cookie or a traybake every day and never get bored. I had to include some classics here like my No-Bake Millionaire's Traybake (page 108) and Raspberry Crumble Bars (page 98), as well as SO many new and fun recipes. My Chocolate Concrete (page 112), Bakewell Slice (page 96), Crinkle Cookies (page 72), or even Lemon Meringue NYC Cookies (page 76)… there are so many exciting bakes in this chapter!

DESSERTS & PUDDINGS

We've all got room for pudding, even after a tasty meal. It's like humans have a separate stomach for dessert. Chocolate Orange Cookie Dough Desserts (page 136), Apple Pie (page 138), Cornflake Tart (page 130), No-Bake Microwave Lemon Pudding (page 144), Peach Sorbet (page 152)… the list goes on.

SWEET TREATS

I love having a sweet little treat to devour, snack on or satisfy a craving and the recipes you can create are never-ending. A few classic fudge recipes, some delectable truffles and sweets, as well as some extra special treats such as Cinnamon Knots (page 168), or Mini Berry Pastries (page 156). A wonderful mix of fruity, chocolatey and fun.

SAVOURY SNACKS & SIDES

We all need something, a little snack sometimes or something easy and fun to serve on the side of our main meal and there are so many choices here. Choose from Homemade Houmous (page 242), a Homemade Cheese Dip and Tortilla Chips (page 247) or Baked Feta and Tomato Dip (page 244), which you can eat with my Crusty Bread recipe (page 240). Or enjoy Dough Balls (page 236), Giant Stuffed Hasselback Potatoes (page 260) or Pizza Quesadilla (page 255).

SAVOURY MEALS

Even though I would eat dessert for starter, main and pudding, we do need dinner first. This section is full of quick, simple super-tasty dishes and I love them all. Frying Pan Pizzas (page 226), 15-Minute Carbonara (page 209), a Chickpea and Spinach Curry (page 218), or even a Honey Garlic Chicken treat (page 204), there are so many delicious options to choose from.

HOW TO USE THIS BOOK...

These recipes are all easy, fun favourites and you will love them. However, to switch things up, I wanted to put them into categories to make it even easier for you to find something to suit you. So check out the symbols you'll see throughout the book to show which type of recipe you are making. Have a look for these:

5 INGREDIENTS OR LESS
Sometimes, you just want to shove a couple of things in a bowl and create something wonderful. You want to have to prep as little as possible and still enjoy a delicious bake, and it really is possible. These recipes will help you create dishes full of flavour for you to devour, but with minimal effort and ingredients.

30 MINUTES OR LESS
We are all frequently pushed for time. We want to be able to cook sweet and savoury recipes as quickly as possible. When I get home from a long day, I want to be able to enjoy something that I have made fresh, there and then. These speedy recipes are perfect for creating a tasty dinner or dessert that won't put you under any stress.

BACK TO BASICS
These recipes are really bringing you back to the basics of cooking and baking on purpose, and are a great place to start. They are popular bakes and ideas that everyone will enjoy, but more original in concept or flavour.

CROWD-PLEASERS
Sometimes, you want to make something to please a lot of people, whether it's your family, your friends, for a party or special occasion. I wanted to bring you recipes that are popular, fun, tasty and still SO easy to make. These recipes will bring you compliments on your baking and cooking skills, but no one needs to know how easy it was to make... right?!

NO-BAKE

We all know I am a very big fan of no-bake recipes, because they are so much easier. If you don't have to use an oven, I am happy. For me, a no-bake recipe can still use a hob, or a microwave, but that's totally fine; you don't have to turn on your entire oven, wait ages for it to heat up, or worry that your oven temperature is wrong. These recipes are lovely to make, and so full of flavour.

ONE-PAN

Whether it's a sweet bake in a 23cm (9in) square dish, or a savoury recipe in a large dish, these recipes work wonders. Throw the ingredients into a dish and cook or layer all things sweet and heavenly into a tin, these recipes are so convenient. I adore anything I can bake in one pan – hardly any equipment needed and practically no washing up!

SMALL BATCH

Not everyone wants to feed a crowd, and I get that. It's nice to be able to make the amount of food to suit you there and then, and a small-batch recipe is ideal. Making up to six portions for sweet bakes and less than four for savoury dishes, these recipes are small-scale on purpose. Of course, you can still increase the quantities to serve more people if you fancy.

SLOW COOKERS AND AIR FRYERS

I love using my slow cooker and air fryer these days, and so many recipes can be adapted to suit them. As an added bonus in this book, make sure you look out for the slow-cooker or air-fryer notes to see how you can adapt a recipe to make in each one, and what changes you may need to make.

AIR FRY

- I use an air fryer that can fit an 18cm (7in) round tin in the basket. If your air fryer is a different shape, you will want to find a tin that is a similar size in volume to an 18cm (7in) round tin. Everything with an air-fryer symbol is cooked on the air-fry function. I don't preheat my air fryer but some may need it, so check the instructions for yours before you start.

SLOW COOKER

- I use a 3.5-litre slow cooker, but a larger one can easily be used.

HELPFUL TIPS

Equipment

Some handy bits you may find useful to make the recipes in this book. (Don't worry, it's not all essential, it's just what I use!)

- Weighing scales
- Baking trays
- Oven thermometer
- Mixing bowls
- Spatulas and whisks
- Measuring spoons
- Timer
- Sieve
- Frying pan
- Round pan
- Piping bags
- Piping nozzles
- 5cm (2in) cookie scoops
- Rolling pin
- Hand whisk
- Stand mixer
- Food processor/blender
- Cake tins – 18cm (7in) round, 20cm (8in) round, 23cm (9in) square, 23cm (9in) tart tin, 23 x 33cm (9 x 13in) traybake tin, 900g loaf tin
- Trifle bowls and dessert bowls
- Baking dish
- Roasting tray

Ingredients

A good core cupboard of ingredients can help so much when baking, especially if you need to whip up something quickly.

- Flours – self-raising, plain, strong white bread
- Sugars – caster, icing, soft light brown, soft dark brown, granulated
- Dairy – butter, baking spread, cheeses, milk, cream
- Eggs – I always use medium size
- Dry baking ingredients – cornflour, cocoa powder, dried yeast, baking powder, bicarbonate of soda, instant coffee
- Baking colourings and flavourings
- Chocolates – 70% dark chocolate, milk, white
- Dried fruits and nuts
- Jams, spreads, condensed milk, tinned caramel
- Store cupboard – pasta, rice, tomatoes (I use tinned and sun-dried), oils, pulses, chickpeas etc
- A selection of spices
- Salt and pepper

Freezing

The general rule for me and freezing is that basically anything can be frozen. I never want to waste a thing!

1. **RAW COOKIE DOUGH CAN BE FROZEN FOR 3+ MONTHS.**
   - Add 2 minutes to the baking time.

2. **FROZEN BAKED GOODS CAN BE KEPT FOR 3+ MONTHS.**
   - Wrap cakes in a double layer of clingfilm and then foil.
   - All other baked goods, such as brownies, cookies and desserts will need to be sealed in a freezer-safe container.
   - Defrost in the fridge if it needs to stay chilled once thawed, such as a cheesecake, or defrost on a work surface if it is stored at room temperature normally.

3. **SAVOURY DISHES AND SNACKS CAN BE PREPPED AND FROZEN BEFORE COOKING AND KEPT FOR 3+ MONTHS.**
   - Increase the cooking time by 5–10 minutes.

4. **SAVOURY DISHES AND SNACKS CAN BE FROZEN, AFTER COOKING AND COOLING, AND KEPT FOR 3+ MONTHS.**
   - Reheat by defrosting in the fridge overnight or in the morning of the day they are needed, and then reheat at 180°C/160°C fan, until piping hot.

Vegan

Vegan Baking Swaps

- **Milk** – For a dairy-free option, I prefer to use almond, soy or other nut milks – it's a straight 1:1 swap.
- **Cream** – There are some good dairy-free alternatives available, you just need to make sure they are full-fat. Or coconut cream also works well.
- **Buttermilk** – Add 15ml of lemon juice to 250ml vegan milk to make 250ml homemade vegan buttermilk.
- **Butter** – Try to find a dairy-free alternative that is as firm as possible. Spreads should be avoided as their oil content is higher to make them softer.
- **Eggs** – Mix 1 tablespoon flax or chia seeds with 3 tablespoons of water to make a good egg replacement in some bakes. Alternatively, 60g applesauce, half a mashed ripe banana or 3 tablespoons of aquafaba are also good swaps.
- **Chocolate** – There are many good dairy-free options out there, but some dark chocolate is naturally vegan, so check the label!
- **Honey** – Maple syrup works wonders.
- **Cheese** – I have often made my savoury dishes vegan using straight swaps. Nutritional yeast is lovely to add to a cheesy dish as it brings the cheesy flavour, on top of using a vegan cheese alternative.
- **Meat** – You can find some brilliant vegan meat alternatives out there now such as fake chicken or sausages, and these all work well. Mushrooms give a good meaty texture, as does pressed tofu.

Gluten free

Gluten-free Baking Swaps

- **Flours** – Most flours have gluten-free alternatives available, and they work well. The texture can vary slightly, but xanthan gum is a useful addition.
- **Xanthan gum** – It can vary, but a good start is about ¼ teaspoon of xanthan gum per 150g of flour.
- **Biscuits** – Again, gluten-free options work perfectly. Add butter to biscuits slowly when making a biscuit base, as some biscuits may need slightly less butter to make a good base.
- **Cornflour** – Some bakes, such as cupcakes, can be improved by using cornflour. A lot of custard powders contain only cornflour and are gluten free. Custard powder can improve the texture of a bake tenfold.
- **Pasta** – Rice and lentil-based pastas are often gluten free, and the gluten-free pasta options work perfectly.

Top Tips

All recipes have full methods and instructions, and even some useful notes, but here are my handy top tips that help with any recipe!

1. **ACCURATE MEASUREMENTS**
Inaccurate measuring of ingredients can cause so many problems! Weighing scales or measuring spoons are vital.

2. **PREHEAT THE OVEN BEFORE USING**
The temperature makes a difference. Sometimes oven thermometers can also save you as ovens can vary SO MUCH.

3. **BE PATIENT**
I know it's annoying, but a cheesecake needs time to set, and you don't want to decorate a warm cake.

4. **READ THROUGH THE RECIPE**
Know in advance what you have to do so there are no surprises.

5. **KNOW YOUR EQUIPMENT**
New equipment can change how a recipe turns out, so sometimes practice makes perfect.

6. **INGREDIENTS**
Make sure that you use the correct ingredients. Lower-fat versions or alternatives can change or even ruin a recipe completely. Switching flavours or decoration can work, however – see my swap suggestions in the recipe notes for ideas and inspiration.

7. **HAVE FUN!**
I know this sounds silly but try not to worry and just have fun.

Cakes, Cupcakes & Muffins

APPLE CRUMBLE CAKE

This light, delicious and easy cake merges a lot of my favourite flavours into one.
A homemade crumble is so easy to make, it's only three ingredients and it's so worth it.
I always use cooking apples for this because by the time the sponges have baked, the apple
has a wonderful texture and marrying that with the light spice of cinnamon and brown sugar
is a dream. A spiced but sweet buttercream frosting sandwiching the two layers together
finishes off this crowd-pleasing cake perfectly. Good to make for a crowd, so perfect
for a relaxed dinner with friends or family.

SERVES: 15

PREP: 30 minutes
BAKE: 55–60 minutes
COOL: 1 hour
DECORATE: 30 minutes
LASTS: 3+ days, at
room temperature

Crumble

120g plain flour
60g caster sugar
60g chilled unsalted butter, cubed

Cake

500g cooking apples (peeled/
    chopped weight)
350g soft light brown sugar
300g unsalted butter, at room
    temperature
300g self-raising flour
6 eggs
1 tsp ground cinnamon

Buttercream

250g unsalted butter, at room
    temperature
500g icing sugar
1 tsp ground cinnamon

Preheat the oven to 180°C/160°C fan and line two deep 20cm (8in)
cake tins with parchment paper.

Add the flour, caster sugar and butter to a bowl and rub together
with your fingertips until the mixture resembles breadcrumbs.
Set aside.

Cube the apples into 2cm (¾in) pieces and pour into a new bowl.
Cover with 50g of the soft light brown sugar and mix.

In a new bowl, beat the butter and remaining light brown sugar
together until combined. Add the flour, eggs and cinnamon and
mix until smooth. Fold through the apples. Divide evenly between
the two lined tins, then sprinkle a layer of crumble onto each cake
(about ½cm/³⁄₁₆in deep). Bake in the oven for 40–45 minutes. Leave
to cool fully in the tins.

Sprinkle any spare crumble mixture onto a lined tray and bake in the
oven for 15 minutes. Leave to cool.

Beat the butter on its own for a few minutes, then add the icing
sugar and cinnamon and mix until fluffy. Transfer to a piping bag
with the piping nozzle of your choice fitted and pipe half onto the
first sponge. Top with the second sponge. Pipe on the rest of the
buttercream and sprinkle with the baked crumble.

NOTES

- *It's important to use cooking apples to give the right texture once baked.*
- *You can use shop-bought crumble mixture instead – buy about 200g.*

MARBLE CAKE

Marble cake is iconic and I grew up adoring it. The marriage of vanilla and chocolate is the best of both worlds, and it's just so easy to bake. I make an easy cake batter, split it in two and flavour one half vanilla and one half chocolate. Dollop and swirl into the tin and bake, then you can decorate to your heart's content. Using the clingfilm trick to decorate is a godsend and it makes the frosting look so fun. Just line the frosting up on a piece of clingfilm, roll this into a sausage, snip the end off, then add to a piping bag and go!

SERVES: 12

PREP: 20 minutes
BAKE: 30–35 minutes
COOL: 1 hour
DECORATE: 20 minutes
LASTS: 3+ days, at room temperature

275g unsalted butter, at room temperature
275g caster sugar
275g self-raising flour
5 eggs
25g cocoa powder
2 tbsp whole milk
1 tsp vanilla extract

Buttercream

200g unsalted butter, at room temperature
400g icing sugar
25g cocoa powder
1 tsp vanilla extract
Sprinkles

Preheat the oven to 180°C/160°C fan and line two 20cm (8in) cake tins with parchment paper.

In a large bowl, beat the butter and sugar together until light and fluffy. Add the flour and eggs and mix together. Divide the mixture evenly between two bowls. Add the cocoa powder and milk to one bowl, and the vanilla extract to the other and mix. Dollop randomly between the two lined tins and swirl slightly together.

Bake in the oven for 30–35 minutes, or until baked through. Leave to cool in the tins for 15 minutes, then remove to a wire rack to cool fully.

Buttercream

Beat the butter on its own for a few minutes to loosen it. Add the icing sugar and mix. Divide the mixture evenly between two bowls. Add the cocoa powder to one bowl, and the vanilla extract to the other and mix.

Grab a large piece of clingfilm and add the two flavours of buttercream in two lines in the middle of the clingfilm. Roll up the clingfilm into a sausage, snip off one end and transfer to a piping bag with the piping nozzle of your choice fitted. Pipe the buttercream onto the cake however you fancy. Decorate with sprinkles.

NOTES

- Jazz up this Marble Cake by playing with flavours – add 2 teaspoons of dissolved coffee to the vanilla mixture, or even swap the vanilla extract for orange extract – delicious!

PEACHES AND CREAM CAKE

Oh, hey there my fruity little beauty... I LOVE YOU. Honestly, this cake is so fresh, so light, so delicious and perfect for any baking day. I adore fruity bakes because you can get such sharp and vibrant flavours shining through in such a simple combination of ingredients. Using tinned peaches means that you can bake this all year round, and the syrup is delicious for drizzling over the top of the baked sponges. I use a freshly whipped cream for the filling and topping as I like how light it is alongside the sponge, and it's so tasty.

SERVES: 12

PREP: 20 minutes
BAKE: 30–35 minutes
COOL: 1 hour
DECORATE: 15 minutes
LASTS: 2–3 days,
in the fridge

250g unsalted butter, at room
temperature
250g caster sugar
250g self-raising flour
5 eggs
1 tsp vanilla extract
300–400g tinned peach slices,
syrup reserved

Decoration

300ml double cream
2 tbsp icing sugar
1 tsp vanilla extract
Extra peach slices (optional)

Preheat the oven to 180°C/160°C fan and line two 20cm (8in) cake tins with parchment paper.

In a bowl, beat the butter and sugar together until light and fluffy. Add the flour, eggs and vanilla extract and mix again until combined. Divide the mixture evenly between the lined tins. Lay the peach slices over the top of each cake.

Bake in the oven for 30–35 minutes. Once baked, drizzle the cakes with the reserved peach syrup and leave to cool fully in the tins.

Decoration

Whip the double cream, icing sugar and vanilla extract until soft peaks form. Spread half over one cake, then top with the second sponge and spread over the rest of the whipped cream. Decorate with extra peach slices if you fancy.

NOTES

- *You can use fresh peaches and a simple homemade syrup instead. Just dissolve 75g caster sugar into 75ml water in a pan, then leave to cool.*

- *You can use any other tinned fruit in the same way.*

VICTORIA SPONGE

When it comes to a Victoria sponge, there are a few ways of doing it. People's opinions on ratios, fillings and so on can vary, but this is my favourite basic method. I like having the sponges a little deeper, so you can get a decent slice of cake, and that for me means a six-egg recipe. I find it best to weigh the six eggs in their shells first, then weigh the sugar, flour and butter to match. The filling is light, sweet and delicate as well, and it's the perfect marriage with the lovely light sponges.

SERVES: 12

PREP: 20 minutes
BAKE: 35+ minutes
COOL: 1 hour
DECORATE: 20 minutes
LASTS: 1–2+ days,
in the fridge

300g unsalted butter, at room
 temperature
300g caster sugar
6 eggs
300g self-raising flour
1 tsp baking powder
2 tsp vanilla extract

Filling
300ml double cream
1 tbsp icing sugar
1 tsp vanilla extract
250g strawberry jam
Icing sugar, to dust

Preheat the oven to 180°C/160°C fan and line two 20cm (8in) cake tins with parchment paper.

In a large bowl, beat the butter and sugar together until light and fluffy. Add the eggs, flour, baking powder and vanilla extract and mix until combined. Divide the mixture equally between the lined tins and bake in the oven for about 35 minutes until baked and golden. Leave to cool in the tins for 15 minutes, then remove to a wire rack to cool fully.

Filling

In a bowl, whip the double cream, icing sugar and vanilla extract together until soft peaks form. Spread the cream over the top of the first sponge.

Carefully spread the jam over the top of the cream, then place the second sponge on top. Dust the cake lightly with icing sugar.

NOTES

- *The cake must be kept in the fridge because of the fresh cream filling, but this can naturally dry out a sponge. Leave the cream filling to the last minute for best freshness!*

- *If you want the cake to last longer, swap the fresh cream filling for a simple vanilla buttercream. Make this by mixing 100g of room-temperature unsalted butter and 200g icing sugar.*

- *You can use a different flavoured jam for the filling, or even fresh fruit if you prefer.*

APPLE FRUIT CAKE

I adore creating simple recipes that are absolutely full of flavour and something that people will want to make over and over again. I've had endless requests for an easy fruit cake, and that's how this delicious recipe was born. Using a slightly spiced dried fruit and apple mixture to flavour the sponge is ideal, as it's so impactful but easy to throw into the bowl, mix and bake. This is a one-layer sponge cake that is perfect to enjoy with a cup of tea on a rainy day, or just something that's fun to make with your kids! An optional drizzle of icing finishes it off perfectly.

SERVES: 10

PREP: 30 minutes
BAKE: 60–70 minutes
COOL: 1 hour
DECORATE: 10 minutes
LASTS: 4+ days, at room temperature

175g unsalted butter, at room temperature
150g soft dark brown sugar
3 eggs
50g honey
200g self-raising flour
2 tsp mixed spice
2 eating apples, peeled and cut into small chunks
100g sultanas
100g raisins
100g dried fruit of choice

Decoration (optional)
75g icing sugar
Pinch of ground cinnamon
1–2 tsp water

Preheat the oven to 180°C/160°C fan and line a deep 20cm (8in) cake tin with parchment paper.

Add the butter, sugar, eggs and honey to a bowl and mix to combine. Add the flour and mixed spice and mix. Fold through the apple chunks, sultanas, raisins and dried fruit. Pour into the lined tin and bake in the oven for 60–70 minutes, or until baked through. Leave to cool fully.

Once cooled, mix the icing sugar, cinnamon and water together to form a thick paste. Drizzle over the cake. Serve with a dollop of freshly whipped cream or custard if you fancy.

NOTES

- *For a deeper flavour, switch the honey to treacle.*
- *The soft dark brown sugar can be swapped to soft light brown sugar for a lighter flavour.*
- *The dried fruit can be replaced with more apple or other dried fruits if you fancy.*
- *You can replace some of the dried fruit with your favourite nuts.*

CARAMEL CARROT CAKE

It's no secret that carrot cake is my most-loved cake, so when you add another of my favourite things, caramel, it just gets even better. I adore the light, moist, spiced flavours of carrot cake, so adding a sweet caramel frosting and swirl takes it up a level but keeps it balanced. Carrot cake is a shove-in-a-bowl, mix-with-a-spoon kind of batter, which is so easy to make and the frosting is smooth and delicious from the caramel. I add texture to this cake with pecans because they go so well with caramel, but they are optional. If you want to use shop-bought caramel, go for it, or you can make your own.

SERVES: 12

PREP: 30 minutes
BAKE: 35–40 minutes
COOL: 1 hour
DECORATE: 30 minutes
LASTS: 3+ days,
at room temperature

225ml sunflower oil
5 eggs
275g soft light brown sugar
300g grated carrots
200g chopped pecans
300g self-raising flour
1½ tsp bicarbonate of soda
1 tsp ground ginger
1 tsp ground cinnamon
1 tsp ground nutmeg

Frosting

200g unsalted butter, at room
   temperature
400g icing sugar
75g caramel sauce

Decoration

50g caramel sauce
Chopped pecans (optional)

Preheat the oven to 180°C/160°C fan and line two deep 20cm (8in) cake tins with parchment paper.

In a large bowl, mix the sunflower oil, eggs, sugar and grated carrots together. Add the chopped pecans, flour, bicarbonate of soda, ginger, cinnamon and nutmeg and mix. Divide equally between the lined tins and bake in the oven for 35–40 minutes. Leave to cool fully in the tins.

Frosting

Beat the butter on its own for a few minutes to loosen it. Add the icing sugar and mix again. Add the caramel sauce and beat on a high speed to combine.

Decoration

Spread half the frosting onto the first sponge and drizzle over half the caramel sauce. Add the second sponge, the remaining frosting and the rest of the caramel. Sprinkle on some chopped pecans if you fancy.

NOTES

- *Leave out the spices in the cake if you prefer.*

COOKIES AND CREAM CAKE FOR TWO

Sometimes you just want a little cake for a small celebration, for pudding, or just because the day ends in 'day', and this bake is the answer. It's a one-layer 15cm (6in) cake with a dollop of topping that's utterly scrumptious. The sponge itself is so easy to put together and bake. The topping is a quick buttercream frosting, with even more cookies and cream flavour added for a little pizzazz. You can also double the quantities and bake in two tins to make a small two-layer cake if you want, it really is that easy!

SERVES: 2

PREP: 15 minutes
BAKE: 25–28 minutes
COOL: 1 hour
DECORATE: 15 minutes
LASTS: 2–3 days,
at room temperature

100g self-raising flour
100g soft light brown sugar
  or caster sugar
½ tsp baking powder
60ml vegetable oil
1 egg
1 tsp vanilla extract
50ml whole milk
4–5 cookies and cream biscuits
  (I use Oreos), chopped

Decoration

50g unsalted butter, at room
  temperature
100g icing sugar
½ tsp vanilla extract
2 cookies and cream biscuits
  (I use Oreos), crushed

Preheat the oven to 180°C/160°C fan and line a 15cm (6in) round tin with parchment paper.

Add the flour, sugar and baking powder to a bowl. Pour in the oil, egg, vanilla extract and milk and stir to combine. Stir through the chopped biscuits. Pour into the lined tin and bake in the oven for 25–28 minutes. Leave to cool fully in the tin.

Decoration

In a large bowl, beat the butter, icing sugar and vanilla extract together until fluffy. Spread the frosting over the top of the cake and decorate with the crushed biscuits.

NOTES

- *To make the sponges chocolate, substitute 25g of the self-raising flour for cocoa powder.*

BROWNIE LOAF CAKE

When brownies and cake marry to make the perfect loaf cake of dreams… Yep, that's right, a Brownie Loaf Cake. This is a similar base recipe to my normal brownies, then I just reduced it slightly to fit into a 900g loaf tin. I swapped the plain flour for self-raising to create a more cake-like base, which isn't quite as dense as a normal brownie. The chocolate frosting is so luxurious to dollop and swirl on top, and I just adore it. You can choose not to decorate the cake, as it's already super chocolatey, but it is chocoholics' heaven, and I love it.

SERVES: 10

PREP: 30 minutes
BAKE: 50–60 minutes
COOL: 4 hours
DECORATE: 30 minutes
LASTS: 4+ days,
at room temperature

150g dark chocolate
150g unsalted butter, at room
  temperature
3 eggs
225g caster sugar
125g self-raising flour
35g cocoa powder
200g chocolate chips of choice

Decoration

100g unsalted butter, at room
  temperature
200g icing sugar
75g dark chocolate, melted
Extra chocolate chips of choice

Preheat the oven to 180°C/160°C fan and line a 900g loaf tin with parchment paper.

In a heatproof bowl, break up the dark chocolate into pieces and add the butter. Melt together in the microwave in short bursts or set the bowl over a pan of simmering water (bain-marie) until smooth. Leave to cool for 5 minutes.

Add the eggs and sugar to a new bowl and whisk until doubled in volume. Fold through the cooled chocolate mixture. Add the flour, cocoa powder and chocolate chips and fold through.

Pour into the lined tin and bake in the oven for 50–60 minutes, or until baked through. Leave to cool fully in the tin.

Decoration

Beat the butter on its own for a couple of minutes to loosen it, then add the icing sugar and mix. Add the melted dark chocolate and beat to combine. Transfer to a piping bag with the piping nozzle of your choice fitted and pipe onto the cooled Brownie Loaf Cake. Decorate with extra chocolate chips.

NOTES

- *It's important to use dark chocolate for the base to make the brownie bake perfectly, but you can use any flavour chocolate chips you like.*

- *You can switch the chocolate chips to chopped nuts in the Brownie Loaf Cake or the decoration, whichever you like.*

STICKY GINGER LOAF CAKE

I adore a ginger cake because it's slightly denser than a sponge, but SO full of flavour. I have had endless requests for a loaf cake version of this, as I have always done a sticky toffee cake… but ginger cake?! Oh, wow. The ginger, cinnamon and nutmeg are wonderful with the additional crystallised ginger for warmth and flavour. Depth and sweetness come from the combination of golden syrup and black treacle, but you can use all of one or the other if you prefer. This easy cake is wonderful served warm with a little butter on, or perfect as a decorated bake.

SERVES: 8

PREP: 15 minutes
BAKE: 50–60 minutes
COOL: 1 hour
LASTS: 4–5+ days,
at room temperature

225g plain flour
2 tsp ground ginger
1 tsp ground cinnamon
1 tsp ground nutmeg
1 tsp bicarbonate of soda
100g crystallised ginger, chopped
125g soft dark brown sugar
125g unsalted butter
125g black treacle
125g golden syrup
2 eggs
100ml whole milk

Decoration

75g icing sugar
½ tsp ground ginger
1–2 tsp water

Preheat the oven to 180°C/160°C fan and line a 900g loaf tin with parchment paper.

Add the flour, ground ginger, cinnamon, nutmeg and bicarbonate of soda to a large bowl with the crystallised ginger and soft dark brown sugar. Mix to combine.

Add the butter, black treacle and golden syrup to a pan and melt together over a low heat. Pour into the dry ingredients and combine. Add the eggs and milk and stir again to combine. Pour into the lined tin and bake in the oven for 50–60 minutes. Leave to cool for 15 minutes before removing from the tin. Then leave to cool fully.

Decoration

Add the icing sugar, ginger and water slowly to a bowl and mix to form a thick paste. Drizzle over the cake.

NOTES

- You can sprinkle over pieces of chopped crystallised ginger to decorate as well.

- If you want a lighter flavour, swap the soft dark brown sugar for soft light brown sugar and use just golden syrup.

SUMMER FRUIT DRIZZLE CAKE

Lemon drizzle is probably one of the most famous cake flavours, and I utterly adore it, but I wanted to make something a little different and a little fruitier. I love berries when they are full of flavour in the summer and could eat them all day every day. Adding a mixture of summer berries to this sponge gives it a delicious taste and moistness, and then creating a smashed berry drizzle topping makes it even better! You can also take this bake to the next level by creating a lightly whipped topping for freshness.

SERVES: 8

PREP: 15 minutes
BAKE: 50–60 minutes
COOL: 1 hour
DECORATE: 15 minutes
LASTS: 2–3+ days,
in the fridge

150g unsalted butter, at room
  temperature
150g caster sugar
225g self-raising flour
3 eggs
1 tsp vanilla extract
175g summer berries

Topping

100g summer berries
100g caster sugar
2 tbsp lemon juice

Preheat the oven to 180°C/160°C fan and line a 900g (2lb) loaf tin with parchment paper.

In a large bowl, cream the butter and sugar together. Add the flour, eggs and vanilla extract and mix again. Fold through the berries and pour into the lined tin. Bake in the oven for 50–60 minutes, or until baked.

Topping

Towards the end of the cake baking, add the berries, sugar and lemon juice to a bowl and slightly mash the fruit and mix together.

Once the cake is baked, prick it lightly with a cake skewer or fork, then pour over the topping mixture. Leave the cake to cool fully.

Serve with whipped cream and some extra berries.

NOTES

- *You can top the cake with whipped cream and extra berries instead of serving them alongside.*

- *I use fresh berries but frozen do work, although it can mean the cake takes a little longer to bake.*

LEMON DRIZZLE TRAYBAKE

This cake is the perfect six-ingredient traybake and is so easy to throw together. Lemon drizzle is always a super popular flavour, and I utterly adore it. Lemon is a very versatile ingredient, as I use it quite a lot in my savoury cooking, too, to bring out flavours, thicken sauces, etc. In the baking world, I add it to as many bakes as possible. This traybake uses just the simplest of ingredients, but they make a big impact and that's what makes it such an easy and amazing bake.

SERVES: 15

PREP: 20 minutes
BAKE: 35–40 minutes
COOL: 1 hour
DECORATE: 15 minutes
LASTS: 3–4+ days,
at room temperature

325g unsalted butter,
   at room temperature
325g caster sugar
325g self-raising flour
6 eggs
Zest of 2 lemons

Drizzle

115ml lemon juice
115g caster sugar

Decoration

75g icing sugar
1–2 tsp lemon juice
Zest of 1 lemon

Preheat the oven to 180°C/160°C fan and line a 23 x 33cm (9 x 13in) traybake tin with parchment paper.

In a large bowl, beat the butter and sugar together until light and fluffy. Add the flour, eggs and lemon zest and mix again. Pour into the lined tin and spread until even. Bake in the oven for 35–40 minutes.

Drizzle

While the sponge is baking, mix the lemon juice and sugar together until combined.

Remove the sponge from the oven, then pour over the drizzle evenly. Leave the cake to cool fully.

Decoration

Mix the icing sugar and lemon juice together to form a thick paste. Drizzle over the cake. Sprinkle on the lemon zest.

NOTES

- *You can switch the lemons to limes (use the zest of 3 limes), or oranges (use the zest of 1–2 large oranges).*

SCHOOL CAKE

School cake is iconic, right? We all know and love it, but if you don't, well, where have you been?! It's probably one of the simplest bakes you can make and have fun with. The sponge is made from five simple everyday ingredients, mixed together and baked into a traybake. You top the cake with a water icing, nice and thick, then sprinkle on some beautiful colourful sprinkles. Of course, if you have a theme, you can adapt the decoration colours or even the sponge colouring to suit! I serve mine with a giant glug of custard because YUMMY.

SERVES: 15+

PREP: 20 minutes
BAKE: 45–50 minutes
COOL: 1 hour
DECORATE: 1 hour
LASTS: 3+ days,
at room temperature

400g unsalted butter,
 at room temperature
400g caster sugar
7–8 eggs
400g self-raising flour
1 tsp vanilla extract

Icing
500g icing sugar
4–5 tbsp water

Decoration
Rainbow sprinkles

Preheat the oven to 180°C/160°C fan and line a 23 x 33cm (9 x 13in) traybake tin with parchment paper.

In a bowl, beat the butter and sugar together until light and fluffy. Add the eggs, flour and vanilla extract and mix until combined. Pour into the lined tin and spread evenly. Bake in the oven for 45–50 minutes, or until baked through. Leave to cool fully in the tin.

Icing
Add the icing sugar to a bowl and gradually add the water, mixing well, until you have a thick paste. Pour over the cake and spread evenly.

Decoration
Sprinkle over your favourite sprinkles, then leave the icing to set for 1 hour.

NOTES

- *For a smaller cake, use a 23cm (9in) square tin and 250g butter, 250g sugar, 5 eggs, 250g flour and ½ teaspoon of vanilla extract and bake for 35 minutes.*

- *Weigh the eggs in their shells, then use whatever is closest to 400g.*

BLUEBERRY ORANGE CUPCAKES

Lemon and blueberry is one of my all-time favourite flavour combinations, but one day I only had oranges so switched to orange and blueberry and oh… my… gosh… YUM. The flavour of these cupcakes is so impactful, plus they are moist and perfect and I just can't get enough. I use orange zest in the cupcake batter and frosting (as the juice may cause this to split). However, you can also use orange extract for even more orange flavour. I then added some blueberry jam inside the cupcakes for even more goodness, but this is optional.

MAKES: 12

PREP: 20 minutes
BAKE: 20–22 minutes
COOL: 1 hour
DECORATE: 20 minutes
LASTS: 3+ days,
in the fridge

150g unsalted butter, at room
    temperature
150g caster sugar
3 eggs
150g self-raising flour
Zest of 1 orange
100g blueberries

Frosting

125g unsalted butter, at room
    temperature
125g icing sugar
250g full-fat soft cheese
Zest of 1 orange

Decoration

100g blueberry jam
Orange slice/orange zest
Blueberries

Preheat the oven to 180°C/160°C fan and get 12 cupcake cases ready on a baking tray.

In a large bowl, beat the butter and sugar together until light and fluffy. Add the eggs, flour and orange zest and combine. Fold through the blueberries.

Split the mixture evenly between the 12 cases. Bake in the oven for 20–22 minutes, or until baked. Leave to cool fully.

Frosting

Beat the butter on its own for a few minutes to loosen it. Add the icing sugar and mix. Add the soft cheese and mix again to combine, then fold through the orange zest.

Decoration

Cut out the middle of each cupcake, add 1 teaspoon of blueberry jam, and pop the middle of each cupcake in again.

Transfer the frosting to a piping bag with the piping nozzle of your choice fitted and pipe onto the cupcakes. Decorate with an orange slice or zest and blueberries.

NOTES

- *For a simple buttercream frosting, use 150g unsalted butter and 300g icing sugar.*

- *The jam is optional or can be switched to marmalade if you fancy something zestier.*

AIR FRY

- *Cook at 160°C for 16–20 minutes.*

CHOCOLATE CUPCAKES

I adore a simple cupcake, chocolate being one of the best, of course. It's always a favourite and a great easy bake to make with kids, or for a party. For these beauties I use a base of melted dark chocolate for a beautiful chocolate flavour, as milk chocolate is a bit too light in cocoa, although it can still work. The chocolate soft cheese frosting is super thick and lovely to decorate with and gives a delicious new twist on the classic buttercream frosting. These are basically chocolate on chocolate, and I'm not mad about it.

MAKES: 12

PREP: 20 minutes
BAKE: 20–22 minutes
COOL: 1 hour
DECORATE: 20 minutes
LASTS: 3+ days,
in the fridge

175g unsalted butter, at room
  temperature
175g soft light brown sugar
3 eggs
175g self-raising flour
175g melted dark chocolate,
  cooled

Frosting

125g unsalted butter, at room
  temperature
100g icing sugar
25g cocoa powder
300g full-fat soft cheese
½ tsp vanilla extract

Decoration

Melted chocolate
Chocolate sprinkles

Preheat the oven to 180°C/160°C fan and get 12 cupcake cases ready on a baking tray.

In a large bowl, beat the butter and sugar together to combine. Add the eggs, flour and melted chocolate and mix until smooth.

Divide evenly between the 12 cases and bake in the oven for 20–22 minutes. Leave to cool fully.

Frosting

Beat the butter on its own for a couple of minutes to loosen it, then add the icing sugar and cocoa powder and mix. Add the soft cheese and the vanilla extract and mix again until smooth. Transfer to a piping bag with the piping nozzle of your choice fitted and pipe onto the cupcakes.

Decoration

Decorate with a drizzle of melted chocolate and sprinkles.

NOTES

- *Try adding some chocolate chips to your cupcakes if you fancy, 100g should work well.*

- *For a lighter flavour, use milk chocolate instead of dark chocolate.*

AIR FRY

- *Cook at 160°C for 16–20 minutes.*

CHOCOLATE RASPBERRY CUPCAKES

Chocolate + raspberry = the dreamiest of dreamy flavours and I cannot get enough of it. Simple chocolate cupcakes can be brought to life with a filling of raspberry ganache, topped with a raspberry coulis buttercream frosting. These may look a little over the top, but honestly, they're not! Use a shop-bought jam or coulis to make your frosting and a wide piping nozzle for a beautiful swirl. An impressive but simple bake for a celebration or party.

MAKES: 12

PREP: 40 minutes
BAKE: 20–22 minutes
COOL: 1 hour
DECORATE: 30 minutes
LASTS: 3+ days,
in the fridge

200g unsalted butter, at room
   temperature
200g soft light brown sugar
4 eggs
150g self-raising flour
50g cocoa powder

Ganache

100g dark chocolate
75ml double cream
75g raspberry jam

Buttercream

200g unsalted butter, at room
   temperature
400g icing sugar
75g raspberry coulis or jam

Decoration

Ganache
Raspberries

Preheat the oven to 180°C/160°C fan and get 12 cupcake cases ready on a baking tray.

In a large bowl, beat the butter and sugar together until light and fluffy. Add the eggs, flour and cocoa powder and combine. Divide evenly between the 12 cases and bake in the oven for 20–22 minutes, or until baked. Leave to cool fully.

Ganache

In a heatproof bowl, break up the dark chocolate into pieces and pour over the double cream. Melt on a low heat in the microwave in 30-second bursts, stirring well, until smooth. Mix through the raspberry jam.

Buttercream

Beat the butter on its own for a few minutes to loosen it. Add the icing sugar and mix, then fold through the coulis or jam.

Decoration

Core out the middle of the cupcakes and fill each one with 1 teaspoon of raspberry ganache. Transfer the buttercream to a piping bag with the piping nozzle of your choice fitted and pipe onto the cupcakes. Add an extra drizzle or blob of ganache. Finish with some raspberries.

NOTES

- *You can add raspberries to the sponges if you want – fold through 150g before baking. Or fold through 150g chocolate chips of your choice.*

- *If you want an easier recipe, just replace the ganache with raspberry jam.*

AIR FRY

- *Cook at 160°C for 16–20 minutes.*

TIRAMISU CUPCAKES

Tiramisu is a classic world-famous dessert, and I am absolutely in love with it. My previous book had a recipe for tiramisu, but after making it endless times I wanted to have fun and experiment by merging two delicious bakes: tiramisu and cupcakes. These cupcakes have a brown sugar coffee base with a tiramisu soaking, then a light and yummy mascarpone coffee frosting that I just want to devour with a spoon.

MAKES: 12

PREP: 20 minutes
BAKE: 20–22 minutes
COOL: 1 hour
DECORATE: 20 minutes
LASTS: 3+ days,
in the fridge

2 tsp instant coffee
2 tsp boiling water
200g unsalted butter, at room
  temperature
200g soft light brown sugar
4 eggs
200g self-raising flour
1 tsp vanilla extract

Syrup

1 tsp instant coffee
50g caster sugar
35ml boiling water
25ml Kahlúa

Frosting

1 tsp instant coffee
1 tsp boiling water
200g mascarpone
100g icing sugar
100ml double cream
25ml Kahlúa
Cocoa powder, for dusting

Preheat the oven to 180°C/160°C fan and get 12 cupcake cases ready on a baking tray.

Dissolve the instant coffee in the boiling water and leave to cool.

In a large bowl, beat the butter and sugar together until light and fluffy. Add the eggs, flour, cooled coffee and vanilla extract and combine. Divide the mixture evenly between the 12 cases and bake in the oven for 20–22 minutes, or until baked.

Syrup

While the cupcakes are baking, add the instant coffee, caster sugar, boiling water and Kahlúa to a bowl and stir to combine and melt the coffee/sugar. Remove the cupcakes from the oven and carefully spoon over the syrup. Leave to cool fully.

Frosting

Dissolve the instant coffee in the water and leave to cool.

Add the mascarpone to a bowl with the icing sugar and double cream and whisk until thick. Add the Kahlúa and dissolved coffee and whisk again. Transfer to a piping bag with the piping nozzle of your choice fitted and pipe the frosting onto the cupcakes.
Dust lightly with cocoa powder and chocolate coated coffee beans, if you fancy, to finish.

NOTES

- *Instead of instant coffee, you can use espresso from a coffee machine if you have one.*

- *If you want alcohol-free cupcakes, just leave out the Kahlúa.*

AIR FRY

- *Cook at 160°C for 16–20 minutes.*

COFFEE AND WALNUT CUPCAKES

When I was little, I didn't really like nuts and I couldn't drink coffee, so these cupcakes sound like my childhood nightmare! However, they are SO moist and tasty I just can't get over it. Sometimes cupcakes can be a bit sickly, or too sweet, but the coffee in the sponge and buttercream gives these a delightful twist of almost bitterness with sweetness. I make my cupcake mix after I have dissolved my coffee, so that it has a chance to cool before using it in the batter. If you want to use an espresso shot, go ahead – especially if it's delicious coffee!

MAKES: 12

PREP: 20 minutes
BAKE: 20–22 minutes
COOL: 1 hour
DECORATE: 20 minutes
LASTS: 3+ days,
at room temperature

2 tsp instant coffee
2 tsp boiling water
150g unsalted butter, at room
    temperature
150g soft light brown sugar
3 eggs
150g self-raising flour
100g walnuts, chopped

Buttercream

2 tsp instant coffee
2 tsp boiling water
150g unsalted butter, at room
    temperature
300g icing sugar

Decoration

50g walnuts, chopped
Sprinkles

Preheat the oven to 180°C/160°C fan and get 12 cupcake cases ready on a baking tray.

Dissolve the coffee in the boiling water and leave to cool.

Beat the butter and sugar together until light and fluffy. Add the eggs, flour and cooled coffee and combine. Fold through the chopped walnuts. Divide the mixture evenly between the 12 cases. Bake in the oven for 20–22 minutes, or until baked. Leave to cool fully.

Buttercream

Dissolve the coffee in the boiling water and leave to cool.

Beat the butter on its own for a few minutes to loosen it. Add the icing sugar and mix. Add the cooled coffee and beat again.

Decoration

Transfer the buttercream to a piping bag with the piping nozzle of your choice fitted and pipe onto the cupcakes. Decorate the cupcakes with chopped walnuts and sprinkles.

NOTES

- *You can use a strong espresso shot from a coffee machine if you prefer.*

- *For coffee cupcakes, just leave out the walnuts.*

AIR FRY

- *Cook at 160°C for 16–20 minutes.*

C

BANANA OAT MUFFINS

These are the sort of muffins that are so easy to throw together, plus they make a good breakfast option, a sweet treat, or also just a tasty bake. It might look like quite a few ingredients, but all you have to do is add them (apart from the chocolate chips) to a food processor or blender and blend until smooth. Then simply stir through the chocolate chips for a chunk of heaven in every bite. I use tulip muffin cases as they're bigger and better, and I decorate with extra oats and choccy chips. Honestly, they're SO GOOD.

MAKES: 12

PREP: 20 minutes
BAKE: 20–25 minutes
COOL: 20 minutes
LASTS: 3+ days,
at room temperature

175g rolled oats, plus extra for
    sprinkling
3 medium ripe bananas
3 eggs
225ml Greek yoghurt
2 tbsp honey
1 tsp baking powder
½ tsp bicarbonate of soda
½ tsp vanilla extract
Pinch of salt
150g chocolate chips of choice

Preheat the oven to 200°C/180°C fan and line a 12-hole muffin tray with tulip muffin cases.

Add all the ingredients, except the chocolate chips, to a food processor or blender and blend together. Stir through the chocolate chips.

Divide the mixture evenly between the 12 cases. Sprinkle over some extra oats and chocolate chips if you fancy and bake the muffins in the oven for 20–25 minutes until golden. Leave to cool slightly and then enjoy.

NOTES

- *Add 25g of cocoa powder to make these chocolate muffins.*

- *Or you can swirl 100–150g of chocolate spread into the mixture in the muffin cases.*

- *Sprinkle with extra chocolate chips to finish, if you fancy.*

AIR FRY

- *Cook at 160°C for 18–22 minutes.*

CHOCOLATE CHIP MUFFINS

Bakery-style chocolate chip muffins are SUCH a popular bake, but sometimes they can be hard to make at home. I have had endless requests for a recipe and, after lots of testing and hundreds of tulip muffin cases later, these are the ones. They're a mix of butter, oil and buttermilk, which sounds like a lot, but it creates perfectly moist muffins and the best rise. I tend to stick to dark chocolate chips, but you can use any you fancy, or even a mixture. I love adding more on top for decoration, plus that extra hit of extra chocolate.

MAKES: 12

PREP: 20 minutes
BAKE: 22–25 minutes
COOL: 30 minutes
LASTS: 3+ days,
at room temperature

75g unsalted butter, melted

75g vegetable oil

175g soft light brown sugar, plus
extra for sprinkling

2 eggs

1 tsp vanilla extract

250g plain flour

1 tsp baking powder

Pinch of salt

125ml buttermilk

200g chocolate chips of choice,
plus extra for sprinkling

Preheat the oven to 200°C/180°C fan and get 12 tulip muffin cases ready on a baking tray.

Add the melted butter, oil and sugar to a bowl with the eggs and vanilla extract and mix until combined. Add the flour, baking powder and salt and mix. Pour in the buttermilk and mix again. Fold through the chocolate chips.

Divide the mixture evenly between the 12 cases. Sprinkle on the extra chocolate chips and extra light brown sugar. Bake in the oven for 22–25 minutes until baked. Leave to cool slightly and enjoy.

NOTES

- *You can use whatever flavour chocolate chips you want – I like using dark chocolate most of the time.*

- *You can make your own buttermilk by using 125ml whole milk and mixing in ½ tbsp of lemon juice.*

AIR FRY

- *Cook at 160°C for 18–22 minutes.*

Cookies & Traybakes

BLACK FOREST COOKIES

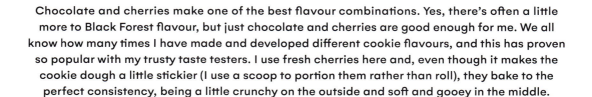

Chocolate and cherries make one of the best flavour combinations. Yes, there's often a little more to Black Forest flavour, but just chocolate and cherries are good enough for me. We all know how many times I have made and developed different cookie flavours, and this has proven so popular with my trusty taste testers. I use fresh cherries here and, even though it makes the cookie dough a little stickier (I use a scoop to portion them rather than roll), they bake to the perfect consistency, being a little crunchy on the outside and soft and gooey in the middle.

MAKES: 10

PREP: 20 minutes
CHILL: 30+ minutes
BAKE: 11–12 minutes
COOL: 30 minutes
LASTS: 3+ days,
at room temperature

175g unsalted butter, at room
temperature
150g soft light brown sugar
100g white granulated sugar
1 egg
1 tsp vanilla extract
250g plain flour
35g cocoa powder
½ tsp baking powder
½ tsp bicarbonate of soda
½ tsp sea salt
200g dark chocolate chips
150g fresh cherries, pitted and
chopped

In a large bowl, beat the butter and both sugars together until creamy. Add the egg and vanilla extract and beat again. Add the flour, cocoa powder, baking powder, bicarbonate of soda and salt and beat until a cookie dough is formed. Add the chocolate chips and chopped cherries and fold together.

Using a tablespoon, scoop 10 cookies onto two large, lined baking trays. Place the trays in the freezer for at least 30 minutes, or in the fridge for 1 hour or so. While the cookie dough is chilling, preheat the oven to 200°C/180°C fan.

Take the cookies out of the freezer or fridge and bake in the oven for 11–12 minutes. Leave to cool on the trays for at least 30 minutes, as they will continue to bake while cooling.

NOTES

- *You can use glacé cherries if you prefer, they'd be delicious! You can also use dried cherries.*

- *Try using other flavours of chocolate chips to change things up.*

AIR FRY

- *Line the base of your air fryer with a piece of parchment paper. Cook at 160°C for 10–12 minutes.*

CHOCOLATE CHIP COOKIES

I have made endless cookie recipes, but I just wanted to create the perfect simple chocolate chip cookie, which means it's also perfect to bake with little ones. This dough is slightly richer than usual as it uses an extra egg yolk, along with more cornflour than normal. The dough requires chilling, but that's okay… it's worth the wait, I promise. I make my cookie dough in a bowl, whack the bowl in the fridge for an hour, or the freezer for 30 minutes, and preheat the oven. I use a 5cm (2in) scoop to portion my cookies, then bake!

MAKES: 15+

PREP: 20 minutes
CHILL: 30+ minutes
BAKE: 10–15 minutes
COOL: 30 minutes
LASTS: 3+ days,
at room temperature

175g unsalted butter, melted and cooled
150g soft light brown sugar
100g granulated sugar
1 egg
1 egg yolk
1 tsp vanilla extract
285g plain flour
½ tsp bicarbonate of soda
50g cornflour
½ tsp sea salt
250g chocolate chips of choice

In a large bowl, mix together the melted and cooled butter and both sugars to combine. Add the egg and egg yolk, along with the vanilla extract, and mix. Add the flour, bicarbonate of soda, cornflour and sea salt and mix until a cookie dough is formed. Fold through the chocolate chips. Chill the dough in the freezer for 30 minutes or the fridge for 1 hour.

While the dough chills, preheat the oven to 200°C/180°C fan and line 2–3 large baking trays with parchment paper.

Using a 5cm (2in) cookie scoop, portion the cookies onto the lined trays. Bake in the oven for 10–15 minutes, then leave to cool fully on the trays.

NOTES

- I love to sprinkle a little sea salt on these cookies once they're out of the oven.

- You can use any chocolate chips, but I especially like using dark chocolate in these cookies.

- If you want a softer cookie, bake for 10–11 minutes and cool on the trays. If you want a crunchier cookie, bake for 13–15 minutes and then cool.

AIR FRY

- Line the base of your air fryer with a piece of parchment paper. Cook at 160°C for 10–12 minutes.

CRINKLE COOKIES

Whenever I see a crinkle cookie, I immediately want to grab one and shove it in my face because they have the most wonderful flavour and texture. I've made them for a few years now but have never published a recipe, which is slightly unfair of me I will admit. So here you go… the requests can stop now! These beauties are fun, full of delicious chocolate flavour, and are a great go-to bake for any cookie craving. These are perfect to make with your kids because you can all get a little messy, but also, they are just so tasty you will want to get involved!

MAKES: 18–20+

PREP: 20 minutes
CHILL: 30 minutes
BAKE: 10 minutes
COOL: 30 minutes
LASTS: 3+ days,
at room temperature

75g cocoa powder
225g caster sugar
75ml sunflower oil
3 eggs
200g plain flour
1 tsp baking powder
Pinch of sea salt
50g icing sugar

In a large bowl, mix the cocoa powder, sugar, oil and eggs together. Add the flour, baking powder and salt and mix until a cookie dough is formed. Chill the bowl in the fridge for 30 minutes.

Preheat the oven to 190°C/170°C fan and line 2–3 large baking trays with parchment paper. Add the icing sugar to a small bowl.

Using a tablespoon, portion the cookies and roll each one into a ball. Then roll each one in the icing sugar. Place each cookie onto the lined trays, spaced well apart from each other.

Bake in the oven for 10 minutes. Leave to cool on the trays and then enjoy.

NOTES

- *If you just want a simple plain chocolate cookie, leave out rolling the cookies in icing sugar.*

AIR FRY

- *Line the base of your air fryer with a piece of parchment paper. Cook at 160°C for 10–12 minutes.*

GINGER COOKIES

Ginger is such a warming and heavenly flavour, and a ginger cookie is the epitome of yum. These use a simple one-bowl cookie dough that is easy to mix together and then bake into beautiful cookies. You must make them immediately! This recipe uses self-raising flour to create a lovely light and chewy texture, but if you want a denser cookie, then plain flour will work as well. The spices bring a warmth to the cookies, and the sugar adds an extra crunch.

MAKES: 18–20+

PREP: 20 minutes
BAKE: 12–14 minutes
COOL: 30 minutes
LASTS: 3+ days,
at room temperature

150g soft light brown sugar
275g self-raising flour
2 tbsp ground ginger
½ tsp ground cinnamon
½ tsp ground nutmeg
1 tsp bicarbonate of soda
Pinch of sea salt
125g unsalted butter, at room
temperature
1 egg
115g golden syrup

Preheat the oven to 190°C/170°C fan and line 2–3 large baking trays with parchment paper. Set 50g of the sugar aside in a small bowl.

In a large bowl, add the flour, ginger, cinnamon, nutmeg, bicarbonate of soda and salt and combine. Add the butter and remaining sugar to a new bowl and beat together. Add the egg and syrup and beat again. Pour in the dry ingredients and mix until a cookie dough is formed.

Using a tablespoon, portion the cookie dough into heaped tablespoons and roll each one into a ball. Then roll each one in a little of the reserved sugar. Place the cookies onto the lined trays, spread slightly apart from each other.

Bake the cookies in the oven for 12–14 minutes, then leave to cool on the trays.

NOTES
- *For a richer flavour, use soft dark brown sugar and replace half of the golden syrup with black treacle.*

AIR FRY
- *Line the base of your air fryer with a piece of parchment paper. Cook at 160°C for 10–12 minutes.*

LEMON MERINGUE NYC COOKIES

Lemon meringue is such an iconic dessert, and cookies are the best, so why would I not try to merge two of my favourite things?! These cookies have a sweetness from the white chocolate chips, but the lemon brings in a zingy fresh flavour that marries so well with the chocolate, and then crunchy meringue adds another level on top again. It's best to use shop-bought meringues here, as you want the super crunchy bits for the cookies, and don't break them up too much when you mix them in.

MAKES: 8

PREP: 20 minutes
CHILL: 30+ minutes
BAKE: 11–12 minutes
COOL: 30 minutes
LASTS: 3+ days,
at room temperature

125g unsalted butter, at room
   temperature
100g soft light brown sugar
75g granulated sugar
1 egg
Zest of 2 lemons
300g plain flour
1½ tsp baking powder
½ tsp bicarbonate of soda
½ tsp sea salt
300g white chocolate chips
50g meringues, crushed

In a large bowl, beat the butter and both sugars together until creamy. Add the egg and lemon zest and beat again. Add the flour, baking powder, bicarbonate of soda and salt and beat until a cookie dough is formed. Add the white chocolate chips and meringues and mix through.

Weigh the cookie dough out into eight balls about 120g each. Chill in the freezer for at least 30 minutes, or in the fridge for 1 hour or so. While the cookies are chilling, preheat the oven to 200°C/180°C fan.

Take the cookies out of the freezer or fridge and divide between two large, lined baking trays.

Bake in the oven for 11–12 minutes. Leave to cool on the trays for at least 30 minutes, as they will continue to bake while cooling.

NOTES

- *You want to use the crunchy meringues you can buy in the shops; you don't want soft marshmallowy ones!*

- *You can use 1-2 teaspoons of lemon extract in place of the lemon zest if you prefer.*

AIR FRY

- *Line the base of your air fryer with a piece of parchment paper. Cook at 160°C for 10–12 minutes.*

PEANUT BUTTER COOKIES

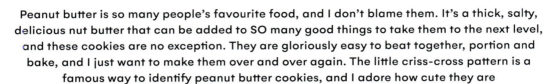

Peanut butter is so many people's favourite food, and I don't blame them. It's a thick, salty, delicious nut butter that can be added to SO many good things to take them to the next level, and these cookies are no exception. They are gloriously easy to beat together, portion and bake, and I just want to make them over and over again. The little criss-cross pattern is a famous way to identify peanut butter cookies, and I adore how cute they are (but they are never too cute not to eat!).

MAKES: 18–20+

PREP: 20 minutes
CHILL: 30+ minutes
BAKE: 10–12 minutes
COOL: 30 minutes
LASTS: 3+ days,
at room temperature

115g unsalted butter, at room
temperature
100g white granulated sugar
100g soft light brown sugar
115g crunchy or smooth peanut
butter
1 egg
200g plain flour
½ tsp baking powder
½ tsp bicarbonate of soda
½ tsp sea salt

In a large bowl, beat the butter and both sugars together until combined. Add the peanut butter and egg and mix again. Add the flour, baking powder, bicarbonate of soda and salt and mix until a cookie dough is formed. Wrap the dough in clingfilm and chill in the fridge for 1 hour or the freezer for 30 minutes.

At the end of the chilling time, preheat the oven to 190°C/170°C fan and line 2–3 baking trays with parchment paper.

Using a tablespoon, portion the cookies and roll each one into a ball. Gently flatten the cookies with a fork in a criss-cross pattern – it can help to lightly dip the fork in flour to stop the cookies sticking.

Bake in the oven for 10–12 minutes. Leave to cool on the trays for 5 minutes and then transfer to wire racks to cool completely.

NOTES

- *If you want your cookies to be softer and chewier, bake them at 170°C/150°C fan for 14–16 minutes.*

AIR FRY

- *Line the base of your air fryer with a piece of parchment paper. Cook at 160°C for 8–10 minutes.*

THUMBPRINT COOKIES

I love creating recipes that are easy to make, delicious and more of an everyday kinda bake, and this is definitely one of those. Thumbprint cookies are a fun recipe to get your kids involved with or to make for a bake sale because they are so adaptable to your favourite flavours, and just so simple to throw together. I use raspberry jam because it's my favourite, but you can add any flavour jam, spread, or curd... and you can flavour the cookie dough if you want as well.

MAKES: 18–20+

PREP: 20 minutes
BAKE: 12–14 minutes
COOL: 30 minutes
LASTS: 3+ days,
at room temperature

175g unsalted butter, at room
 temperature
175g caster sugar
1 egg
1 tsp vanilla extract
275g plain flour
½ tsp baking powder
½ tsp sea salt
60g raspberry jam

Preheat the oven to 190°C/170°C fan and line 2–3 large baking trays with parchment paper.

In a large bowl, beat the butter and sugar together until combined. Add the egg and vanilla extract and mix again. Add the flour, baking powder and salt and mix until a cookie dough is formed.

Using a tablespoon, portion the cookies and roll each one into a ball. Using your thumb or the handle of a large utensil, carefully press an indentation into each cookie, then spoon a small amount of jam into the hole. Place the cookies onto the lined trays, spaced well apart from each other.

Bake in the oven for 12–14 minutes. Leave to cool on the trays for 10 minutes, then cool fully on a wire rack.

NOTES

- *Any flavour jam can be used.*

- *Try flavouring the cookie dough with the zest of 1–2 lemons.*

AIR FRY

- *Line the base of your air fryer with a piece of parchment paper. Cook at 160°C for 10–12 minutes.*

BANANA BREAD BLONDIES

Banana bread is such a popular bake and because it is so iconic, I wanted to merge it with another love of mine: blondies. This beautiful traybake is the perfect level of banana bread density and sweet and caramel-y blondie. The mashed bananas in the blondie mixture replace the eggs and create the texture you are after, then a swirl of caramel brings a delicious flavour and the chocolate chips are just a must. I decorated mine just as I would a banana bread, with even more banana. All I can say is that these blondies are elite.

MAKES: 16

PREP: 20 minutes
BAKE: 25–30 minutes
COOL: 1 hour
SET: 2+ hours
LASTS: 4+ days,
at room temperature

200g unsalted butter, melted and cooled
125g white granulated sugar
125g soft light brown sugar
3 bananas, mashed
1 tsp vanilla extract
275g plain flour
1 tbsp cornflour
200g dark chocolate chips
100g caramel sauce
2 bananas, sliced lengthwise

Preheat the oven to 180°C/160°C fan and line a 23cm (9in) square tin with parchment paper.

In a large bowl, mix the melted butter and both sugars together until smooth. Add the mashed bananas and vanilla extract and mix again until smooth. Add the flour, cornflour and chocolate chips and mix. Pour into the lined tin.

Drizzle over the caramel sauce and swirl through the mixture. Lay the sliced bananas over the top randomly.

Bake in the oven for 25–30 minutes until there is a small wobble in the middle of the tin. Leave to cool fully in the tin. Then, set the blondies in the fridge for at least 2 hours for a perfectly set blondie.

NOTES

- *The bananas on top are optional, but they add a lovely touch.*

- *For a different flavour, you can easily swap the caramel for another spread, such as chocolate hazelnut or speculoos.*

AIR FRY

- *Halve the recipe and pour into an 18cm (7in) round tin. Cook at 160°C for 14–16 minutes.*

MINT CHOCOLATE BROWNIES

Mint and chocolate make one of the best flavour combinations, right?! RIGHT?! The thick and fudgy brownie, with a creamy mint filling topped with a chocolate butter ganache is the best of the best all shoved together. It may seem like a lot of steps, but honestly all the stages are very easy to achieve and it's worth the cooling and setting time, I promise!

MAKES: 16

PREP: 30 minutes
BAKE: 25–30 minutes
COOL: 1 hour
SET: 3–4 hours
LASTS: 3+ days,
in the fridge

200g dark chocolate
200g unsalted butter, at room
 temperature
4 eggs
275g caster sugar
100g plain flour
50g cocoa powder
1 tsp peppermint extract

Filling

100g unsalted butter, at room
 temperature
200g icing sugar
1–2 tsp peppermint extract
Green food colouring (optional)
2–3 tbsp whole milk

Topping

200g dark chocolate
100g unsalted butter, at room
 temperature

Preheat the oven to 180°C/160°C fan and line a 23cm (9in) square baking tray with parchment paper.

In a heatproof bowl, break up the dark chocolate into pieces and add the butter. Melt together in the microwave in short bursts or set the bowl over a pan of simmering water (bain-marie) until smooth. Leave to cool to room temperature.

In a new bowl, whisk the eggs and sugar together for a few minutes until doubled in volume and pale. Fold through the chocolate mix, then fold through the flour, cocoa powder and peppermint extract.

Pour into the lined tin and bake in the oven for 25–30 minutes (until there is an ever-so-slight wobble in the middle). Leave the brownies to cool completely in the tin.

Filling

Add the butter to a bowl and beat until smooth. Add the icing sugar and peppermint extract and mix. Add a small amount of green food colouring and the milk and mix until smooth. Spread onto the cooled brownie.

Topping

In a heatproof bowl, break up the dark chocolate into pieces and add the butter. Melt together in the microwave in short bursts or set the bowl over a pan of simmering water (bain-marie) until smooth. Pour over the filling layer.

Set the brownies in the fridge for 3–4 hours, then slice and enjoy.

NOTES

- *You can add chocolate chips to the brownie if you want – I'd add 200g of your flavour choice.*

- *If you want them slightly less minty, leave out the peppermint extract from the brownies.*

CHOCOLATE HAZELNUT BROWNIES

I am addicted to brownies, and after I accidentally bought a massive tub of chocolate hazelnut spread (and by accident, I mean purposely went to the shop to buy), I knew I had some experiments to complete. I love all my brownie recipes, but these are so easy to make – you only need one bowl, and the mix is made in 30 seconds or less, then you just bung it in the oven and bake. I top these with chocolate sweets, which is entirely optional, but delicious. You can also have fun using other spreads, such as speculoos or plain chocolate spread.

MAKES: 9

PREP: 10 minutes
BAKE: 20 minutes
COOL: 1 hour
LASTS: 4+ days,
at room temperature

400g chocolate hazelnut spread
  (I use Nutella)

3 eggs

75g plain flour

9 chocolates (I use Ferrero
  Rocher – optional)

Preheat the oven to 180°C/160°C fan and line a 20cm (8in) square tin with parchment paper.

Add the chocolate hazelnut spread, eggs and flour to a large bowl and mix thoroughly with a spatula. Pour into the lined tin and bake in the oven for 20 minutes.

Remove from the oven and press in the chocolates, if using. Leave to cool fully and enjoy.

NOTES

- *You can use any chocolate spread you want.*

- *If you want the brownies to be more cake-like in texture, use self-raising instead of plain flour.*

AIR FRY

- *Reduce the recipe by one third and pour into an 18cm (7in) round tin. Cook at 160°C for 14–16 minutes.*

SPECULOOS BLONDIES

Blondies are one of my favourite bakes, and when you marry them with speculoos I adore them even more. My base blondie mixture features varying ingredients that are quite different from my brownie but work together SO well. I shove in a load of white chocolate chips to bring the white chocolate sweetness without being too much. The perfect way to bake these blondies is until there is an ever-so-slight wobble in the middle of the tin, then let them cool and set in the fridge. The speculoos spread will help create the perfect fudgy texture. These are one of my friends' favourite easy recipes.

MAKES: 16

PREP: 20 minutes
BAKE: 25–30 minutes
COOL: 1 hour
SET: 2+ hours
LASTS: 4+ days,
at room temperature

200g unsalted butter, melted
125g white granulated sugar
125g soft light brown sugar
3 eggs
1 tsp vanilla extract
275g plain flour
1 tbsp cornflour
200g white chocolate chips
100g speculoos biscuits (I use Biscoff), broken into pieces
250g speculoos spread (I use Biscoff)

Preheat the oven to 180°C/160°C fan and line a 23cm (9in) square tin with parchment paper.

Add the melted butter and both sugars to a bowl and mix until smooth. Add the eggs and vanilla extract and mix again until smooth. Add the flour, cornflour and mix. Add the chocolate chips and biscuits and mix through. Pour into the lined tin. Drizzle over the speculoos spread and swirl through the mixture.

Bake in the oven for 25–30 minutes until there is a small wobble in the middle of the tin.

Leave to cool fully in the tin. Then chill the blondies in the fridge for at least 2 hours for a perfectly set blondie.

NOTES

- *The fridge setting trick helps if your blondies are slightly underbaked. If you find your blondies are cakey, then they have been overbaked, so need less baking time next time.*

AIR FRY

- *Halve the recipe and pour into an 18cm (7in) round tin. Cook at 160°C for 14–16 minutes.*

GINGER SLICE

I recommend this six-ingredient bake to anyone who wants a delicious and simple recipe to make that is always a popular eat. It has a warming ginger shortbread base and the topping is also easy – just melt the butter, syrup and ginger in a pan and beat in the sugar, then pour over the biscuit base and set. Honestly, the steps are very simple, and despite the cool and setting times, it's SO easy. I love it as it is, or even serving it with a little custard for a pudding…

MAKES: 16

PREP: 20 minutes
BAKE: 25–30 minutes
SET: 2–3+ hours
LASTS: 4+ days,
at room temperature
or in the fridge

200g unsalted butter, at room
  temperature
100g caster sugar
300g plain flour
2 tsp ground ginger

Topping

150g unsalted butter
75g golden syrup
5 tsp ground ginger
200g icing sugar

Preheat the oven to 200°C/180°C fan and line a 23cm (9in) square tin with parchment paper.

In a large bowl, cream the butter and sugar together, then add the flour and ginger and mix again. Press into the base of the lined tin. Bake in the oven for 25–30 minutes, or until golden and allow to cool.

Topping

Add the butter, syrup and ginger to a pan over a medium heat and melt together until smooth. Take the pan off the heat and mix in the icing sugar. Spread over the top of the base and leave to set for at least 2–3 hours.

NOTES

- *To make it even more ginger-y, add some chopped crystallised ginger into the topping mix.*

BAKEWELL SLICE

Bakewell is one of my favourite flavours in the world, and I do not get bored of it. I have made endless Bakewell-inspired bakes but have never actually given you my Bakewell Slice recipe until now... Honestly, it was worth the wait. This recipe embodies everything I adore about the combination of almond and fruit, and I have made this so many times I cannot count. I use shop-bought pastry, but you can make your own if you want. I use cherry flavours, but you can swap to raspberry or even strawberry if you prefer. Serve with a giant pour of custard, because why would you not?!

MAKES: 16

PREP: 30 minutes
BAKE: 35–40 minutes
COOL: 2 hours
LASTS: 4+ days,
at room temperature
or in the fridge

1 x sheet of shortcrust pastry

Filling

200g unsalted butter, at room
  temperature, plus extra for
  greasing
200g caster sugar
150g self-raising flour,
  plus extra for dusting
150g ground almonds
1 tsp almond extract
4 eggs
250g cherry jam
200g fresh cherries,
  destoned and halved
35g flaked almonds

Preheat the oven to 200°C/180°C fan and grease and flour the base and sides of a 23cm (9in) square traybake tin.

Unroll the pastry and roll it out into a 30cm (12in) square. Lift into the tin, pushing into the base and sides. Chill for 15 minutes while the oven finishes preheating, and then prick the bottom with a fork all over. Line the pastry with a piece of parchment paper and fill with baking beans.

Bake in the oven for 15 minutes, then remove the beans and paper and bake for a further 5 minutes.

Filling

Put the butter and sugar into a bowl and beat until creamy. Add the flour, ground almonds, almond extract and eggs and mix again until combined.

Spread the jam carefully over the base of the pastry and sprinkle over the cherries. Pour over the cake topping and spread.

Reduce the oven temperature to 180°C/160°C fan. Sprinkle the flaked almonds on top, then bake in the oven for 35–40 minutes. Once baked, leave to cool fully in the tin.

NOTES

- You can make your own pastry – just double the recipe on page 130.

- You don't have to add the cherries to the middle, you can use them for decoration instead or leave them out.

- For a finishing touch, you could mix together 75g icing sugar with 1–2 teaspoons of water to form a thick paste, then drizzle this over the cooled slices.

RASPBERRY CRUMBLE BARS

Say hello to some of the most delicious bits of heaven you will ever eat ... These bars are heavenly and just so incredibly moreish and scrumptious. Traybakes can come in many forms, such as brownies, blondies, cookie bars, flapjacks and so on. These Raspberry Crumble Bars are a new traybake to add to the list of goodness. An oaty crumble is easy to rub together, and mashing the fruity filling is also incredibly quick. As always, these bake in a 23cm (9in) square tin, as I find it the perfect size for baking a sweet traybake.

MAKES: 16

PREP: 30 minutes
BAKE: 30–35 minutes
COOL: 1–2 hours
LASTS: 3+ days,
in the fridge

175g rolled oats
200g plain flour
150g soft light brown sugar
½ tsp baking powder
175g unsalted butter,
  cold and cubed

Filling

450g fresh raspberries
150g raspberry jam
1 tbsp lemon juice
1 tbsp cornflour

Preheat the oven to 200°C/180°C fan and line a 23cm (9in) square tin with parchment paper.

Add the oats, flour, sugar, baking powder and unsalted butter to a bowl. Rub the ingredients together with your fingertips until the mixture resembles breadcrumbs.

Add the raspberries, jam, lemon juice and cornflour to another bowl. Mash the ingredients together until they are combined but the raspberries still have some texture.

Add 500g of the base mixture into the lined tin and press down firmly. Pour over the raspberry mixture. Sprinkle over the remaining base mixture.

Bake in the oven for 30–35 minutes until golden brown. Leave to cool fully in the tin.

NOTES

- *The raspberries can be swapped for other berries, such as blackberries, blueberries, strawberries or even a mixture.*

- *Adding 1 teaspoon of ground ginger or cinnamon to the base mixture gives a wonderful warmth.*

- *If you want a fresher taste, add the zest of 1 lemon to the base.*

COOKIE DOUGH BARS

When baking something cookie-related, it's always a common joke that the cookie dough is better raw, and even though I adore a baked cookie I can't deny that the dough really is delicious. So I thought making a Cookie Dough Bar would solve all of my cookie dough cravings. This thick cookie dough is gloriously full of chocolate chips and topped with a thick chocolate ganache, so it just gets even better. It's an easy treat to throw together and enjoy with friends and family.

MAKES: 16

PREP: 25 minutes
SET: 4+ hours
LASTS: 4+ days,
at room temperature
or in the fridge

125g unsalted butter, at room
   temperature
125g soft light brown sugar
397g tin condensed milk
2 tsp vanilla extract
400g plain flour, heated and
   cooled
½ tsp sea salt
200g chocolate chips of choice

Topping

150g milk chocolate
150g dark chocolate
150g double cream

Line a 23cm (9in) square tin with parchment paper.

In a bowl, mix the butter and sugar together to combine. Add the condensed milk and vanilla extract and mix again. Add the heated and cooled flour, sea salt and chocolate chips and mix again.

Press this cookie dough into the bottom of the lined tin, evenly.

Topping

Add the milk and dark chocolates and double cream to a heatproof bowl. Heat in the microwave on low, in 30-second bursts, stirring well each time, until smooth.

Pour this over the cookie dough, then set the bars in the fridge for at least 4 hours, but preferably overnight. Slice and enjoy.

NOTES

- *You can use any chocolate chips you fancy in the cookie dough.*

- *It is always recommended to heat-treat the flour on a baking tray in the oven at 200°C/180°C fan for 5 minutes and let it cool completely before using.*

GRANOLA BARS

Granola is a classic bake to crack, and creating a basic granola bar is something I have always wanted to do. I love baking these and chopping them into bite-sized pieces for a little sweet treat, but mainly I bake these into bars for a snack or breakfast on the go. I fill mine with a variety of chopped nuts, dried fruit and seeds from the mixed packets, but it's more of a guide to the quantities. If you wanted to do all almonds, raisins and pumpkin seeds, that works as well. Press them down firmly into the lined tin, bake and enjoy.

MAKES: 16

PREP: 15 minutes
BAKE: 25–30 minutes
COOL: 1 hour
LASTS: 4+ days,
at room temperature

125g unsalted butter

100g soft light brown sugar

75g honey

275g rolled oats

1 tsp ground cinnamon

100g chopped nuts (I use pecans, cashews and almonds)

100g dried fruit (I use raisins and cranberries)

100g seeds (I use sunflower seeds)

Preheat the oven to 180°C/160°C fan and line a 23cm (9in) square baking tray with parchment paper.

Add the butter, sugar and honey to a pan over a low heat and cook until the butter has melted.

Add the oats, cinnamon, chopped nuts, dried fruit and seeds to a large bowl and mix. Pour in the melted butter mixture and stir again.

Tip into the lined tin and press down firmly.

Bake in the oven for 25–30 minutes. Leave to cool in the tin, then slice.

NOTES

- *Big, rolled oats are best; porridge oats may make a softer bake.*

AIR FRY

- *Halve the recipe and pour into an 18cm (7in) round tin. Cook at 160°C for 14–16 minutes.*

LEMON AND COCONUT FLAPJACKS

Flapjacks are such a classic bake that it seems silly not to create an even more delicious version of them. Lemon and coconut make such a wonderful flavour combination that I want to develop it more and more, and these flapjacks are the perfect place to start. Adding desiccated coconut and lemon zest to the flapjacks creates a zingy and light taste that is so scrumptious, and when you top these with a little lemon sugar drizzle, they just get even better. Easy, sweet and tangy.

MAKES: 16

PREP: 20 minutes
BAKE: 22–25 minutes
COOL: 2 hours
DECORATE: 15 minutes
LASTS: 4+ days,
at room temperature

200g unsalted butter
200g soft light brown sugar
200g honey
400g rolled oats
Zest of 2 lemons
100g desiccated coconut

Drizzle

75g icing sugar
1–2 tsp lemon juice

Preheat the oven to 180°C/160°C fan and line a 23cm (9in) square baking tray with parchment paper.

Add the butter, sugar and honey to a pan and melt over a low heat until the butter has melted.

Add the oats to a bowl with the lemon zest and desiccated coconut and mix. Pour in the melted butter mixture and stir to combine. Press the mixture into the base of the tin, pressing down as much as you can.

Bake in the oven for 22–25 minutes. Leave the flapjacks to cool fully in the tin.

Drizzle

Mix the icing sugar and lemon juice together to form a thick paste, then drizzle over the flapjacks. Leave to set for around 30 minutes, then portion.

NOTES

- You can add a layer of 200g lemon curd to the middle of the flapjacks if you like. Set the flapjacks in the fridge after cooling, as they may be slightly softer with the filling.

- The drizzle is optional.

- Switch the honey to golden syrup if you like.

AIR FRY

- Halve the recipe and pour into an 18cm (7in) round tin. Cook at 160°C for 14–16 minutes.

NO-BAKE MILLIONAIRE'S TRAYBAKE

So we all know how obsessed I am with all things millionaire's shortbread, right?! However, I have had endless requests for a super-easy no-bake version… so here it is. A biscuit base with shortbread, a caramel made in the microwave, and chocolate. As a millionaire's shortbread usually has a baked shortbread base, I thought I would make it no-bake by simply using a basic biscuit base made from shortbread biscuits and butter, more like a cheesecake. I made the rest of the traybake no-bake by using a microwave. For me, a microwave doesn't count as baking, as you don't have to turn on the oven!

MAKES: 16

PREP: 45 minutes
SET: 2 hours
DECORATE: 20 minutes
LASTS: 4–5+ days,
at room temperature
or in the fridge

400g shortbread biscuits
150g unsalted butter, melted

Caramel

200g unsalted butter
3 tbsp caster sugar
4 tbsp golden syrup
397g tin condensed milk

Decoration

200g white chocolate
100g dark chocolate

Line a 23cm (9in) square tin with parchment paper.

Blitz the biscuits to a fine crumb in a food processor or crush in a bowl with a rolling pin. Add the melted butter and mix together. Press firmly into the base of the lined tin and chill while you make the caramel.

Caramel

Add the butter, sugar, golden syrup and condensed milk to a large heatproof bowl. Heat in the microwave on high in 1-minute bursts, stirring well and carefully each time, until the caramel has thickened and turned golden. This can take 10–15 minutes.

Once golden and thick, pour over the shortbread base and leave to set in the fridge for 1 hour.

Decoration

In two heatproof bowls, break up each chocolate into pieces. Melt separately in the microwave in short bursts or set the bowls over a pan of simmering water (bain-marie) until smooth. Pour over the set caramel randomly and swirl together. Set in the fridge for 1 hour, then portion and enjoy.

NOTES

- *The cooking time can vary for the caramel as microwaves have different levels of power.*

- *Make sure the bowl is LARGE so that the caramel doesn't overflow.*

- *The caramel will get VERY hot during the cooking process, so be careful.*

- *You can use any chocolate you want for the decoration.*

CHOCOLATE CONCRETE

I adore old school classics; we all know this. And Chocolate Concrete?! Probably one of my most highly requested recipes ever. It's an addictive bake because it's so simple, and anything from my childhood wins me over. This beautiful recipe is an easy four-ingredient bake that is effortless to mix, bake and enjoy. Of course, for some people, the classic version means serving it with pink custard, so there are notes on that below... I hope you love this bake as much as I do, because it really is next-level easy.

MAKES: 16

PREP: 20 minutes
BAKE: 20–23 minutes
COOL: 1 hour
LASTS: 4+ days,
at room temperature

250g plain flour
200g caster sugar, plus extra
   for sprinkling
50g cocoa powder
125g unsalted butter

Preheat the oven to 180°C/160°C fan and line a 23cm (9in) square baking tray with parchment paper.

In a large bowl, add the flour, sugar and cocoa powder and mix together.

Add the butter to a pan, or heatproof bowl in the microwave, and melt. Mix the melted butter and the dry ingredients with your hands until a wet sandy dough is formed. Tip this mixture into the tin and press down firmly – I find a lightly floured spoon helpful for this, or floured hands. Brush the surface of the concrete with water and sprinkle on an extra 2–3 teaspoons of sugar.

Bake in the oven for 20–23 minutes. Leave to cool, then slice and enjoy.

NOTES

- *You can serve this with pink custard by mixing 500ml strawberry-flavoured milk with 75g custard powder and stirring them together over a medium heat until thickened. Sweeten it with 1–3 teaspoons of sugar if you fancy.*

NO-BAKE COCONUT TIFFIN

No-bake traybakes are the perfect one-pan dish because there is no oven required,
you can have fun making them and often get covered in chocolate, and they are just so easy.
I love a tiffin because they're super chocolatey, they are easy to adapt to whatever flavours
you prefer (as always, use your favourite nuts/dried fruits, I just use my recipe as a suggestion
and guide to weights), and then mix to your heart's content. I top mine with a delicious
coconut cream-based chocolate ganache topping, which is optional,
but takes it up another level again.

MAKES: 16

PREP: 20 minutes
SET: 3+ hours
LASTS: 4+ days,
at room temperature
or in the fridge

150g golden syrup
150g unsalted butter
400g dark chocolate, chopped
200g digestive or oat biscuits,
   chopped
75g desiccated coconut
125g raisins
125g dried cherries

Topping

250g dark chocolate
100g coconut cream
Desiccated coconut

Line a 23cm (9in) square baking tray with parchment paper.

Melt the golden syrup and butter gently in a pan over a low heat.
When the butter and syrup have melted fully and started to bubble
slightly, turn off the heat and add the chopped chocolate and stir
until the chocolate has melted.

Pour the digestive biscuits, coconut, raisins and cherries into a
large bowl and pour the chocolate/syrup mixture on top. Mix the
ingredients together thoroughly until they are all coated well. Pour
into the tin and press down very firmly.

Topping

In another bowl, melt together the dark chocolate and coconut
cream and stir until smooth. Pour it on top of the tiffin, then sprinkle
on some extra coconut. Leave to set in the fridge for 3–4 hours.

Once set, carefully remove from the tin and cut into pieces.

NOTES

- *You can switch up the dried fruits or replace them with your favourite
chopped nuts.*

- *You can use just-melted chocolate for the topping if you wish or use
double cream instead of the coconut cream.*

Desserts & Puddings

PEANUT BUTTER JELLY CHEESECAKE

Peanut butter and jelly make an absolutely iconic combination, and it's time for the cheesecake version. With a peanut biscuit base, a crunchy peanut butter filling and a jelly topping, you just can't beat it! Usually, I would use jam as the jelly part of a PB&J recipe, but this time it is actually jelly, and I went for raspberry. This mixture of peanut butter cheesecake and raspberry jelly is just SO good and it makes for an easy show-stopping dessert for any occasion. The decoration is so simple with some raspberries and peanuts, and it's perfection on a plate.

SERVES: 12–15+

PREP: 30 minutes
SET: 5–6+ hours
DECORATE: 15 minutes
LASTS: 3+ days,
in the fridge

Jelly

½ x packet raspberry jelly
125ml boiling water
125ml cold water

Base

300g digestive biscuits
50g unsalted peanuts, finely
    chopped
125g unsalted butter, melted

Cheesecake

500g full-fat soft cheese
75g icing sugar
250g peanut butter
1 tsp vanilla extract
300ml double cream

Decoration

Raspberries
Chopped peanuts

Jelly

Add the jelly cubes to a jug with the boiling water and stir to dissolve. Stir through the cold water and leave to cool for 15 minutes while you make the base.

Base

Blitz the biscuits and peanuts to a fine crumb in a food processor or crush in a bowl with a rolling pin. Add the melted butter and mix together. Press into the base of a deep 20cm (8in) springform cake tin.

Cheesecake

In a large bowl, whisk the soft cheese, icing sugar, peanut butter and vanilla extract together. Add the double cream, whip again until thick (or whip separately and fold through). Pour into the tin and smooth over.

Carefully pour over the jelly. Set in the fridge for 5–6 hours, or preferably overnight.

Decoration

Once set, remove carefully from the tin. Sprinkle on some raspberries and chopped peanuts if you wish.

NOTES

- *You can fold through some raspberries into the cheesecake mixture – I'd use 150g.*

- *Both smooth and crunchy peanut butter work well.*

BOURBON BISCUIT CHEESECAKE

Bourbon biscuits are utterly iconic, and they make the best theme for a cheesecake. Using the biscuits as the base and the sides, then filling the middle with a silky, no-bake, chocolate cheesecake filling is just delicious on top of delicious, and I cannot get enough. This recipe is incredibly easy to put together but is a showstopper that will wow everyone when you bring it out for dessert. You can adapt and change the recipe according to your preferences by using different chocolates for the filling, or even swapping it for a custard-cream shell!

SERVES: 12–15+

PREP: 30 minutes
SET: 5–6+ hours
DECORATE: 15 minutes
LASTS: 3+ days,
in the fridge

300g bourbon biscuits
85g unsalted butter, melted

Cheesecake

15–20 bourbon biscuits
200g milk chocolate
500g full-fat soft cheese
75g icing sugar
1 tsp vanilla extract
300ml double cream

Decoration

150ml double cream
2 tbsp icing sugar
Biscuit crumbs
Chocolate curls

Blitz the biscuits to a fine crumb in a food processor or crush in a bowl with a rolling pin.

Add the melted butter and mix together. Press into the base of a deep 20cm (8in) springform cake tin.

Cheesecake

Press the whole biscuits into the biscuit base around the edge of the cake tin.

Melt the milk chocolate until smooth. In a large bowl, whisk the soft cheese, icing sugar and vanilla extract together. Add the melted milk chocolate and whisk together. Finally, add the double cream and whip again until thick (or whip separately and fold through). Pour into the tin, inside the ring of biscuits and smooth over. Set in the fridge for 5–6 hours, or preferably overnight.

Decoration

Remove the cheesecake from the tin.

In a large bowl, whip the cream and icing sugar together. Transfer to a piping bag fitted with the piping nozzle of your choice, then pipe onto the cheesecake. Decorate with biscuit crumbs and chocolate curls.

NOTES

- *You can use other biscuits, such as custard creams, and leave out the chocolate in the cheesecake mixture.*

- *Try swapping the milk chocolate for dark chocolate if you want a richer taste.*

KEY LIME CHEESECAKE

I love having recipe requests for bakes I have wanted to post for so long. This beautiful cheesecake is simple but so tasty. I will admit, this recipe could be better if I could find key limes more easily… However, even with the classic limes that you can buy in the supermarket, the zingy fresh and sharp flavour is absolutely delightful. The cheesecake features a small amount of soured cream as well as the double cream to help increase the flavour, and it's so good. A sweetened whipped cream topping is my go-to – it just works!

SERVES: 12

PREP: 30 minutes
SET: 5–6+ hours
DECORATE: 20 minutes
LASTS: 3+ days,
in the fridge

300g digestive biscuits
125g unsalted butter, melted

Cheesecake

500g full-fat soft cheese
100g icing sugar
75ml lime juice
Zest of 2 limes
150ml double cream
100ml soured cream

Decoration

150ml double cream
1 tbsp icing sugar
Lime slices
Lime zest
Biscuit crumbs

Blitz the biscuits to a fine crumb in a food processor or crush in a bowl with a rolling pin. Add the melted butter and mix together until it resembles wet sand in texture. Press into the base of a 20cm (8in) springform cake tin.

Cheesecake

In a large bowl, whisk the soft cheese, icing sugar, lime juice and zest together until combined.

Pour in the double cream and soured cream and whisk until thickened. Alternatively, whisk the double cream and soured cream in a separate bowl and then fold through the cheesecake filling. Spread the mixture over the biscuit base. Set in the fridge for at least 5–6 hours.

Decoration

Remove the cheesecake from the tin and place on a serving plate. Whip the double cream and icing sugar together until soft peaks form. Transfer to a piping bag fitted with your choice of nozzle and pipe onto the cheesecake however you fancy. Decorate with slices of lime and a sprinkling of zest and biscuit crumbs.

NOTES

- *Key limes are the best limes to use, but they're hard to find. Regular limes work absolutely fine.*

CHOCOLATE CHIP CHEESECAKE BARS

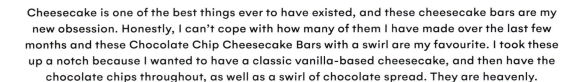

Cheesecake is one of the best things ever to have existed, and these cheesecake bars are my new obsession. Honestly, I can't cope with how many of them I have made over the last few months and these Chocolate Chip Cheesecake Bars with a swirl are my favourite. I took these up a notch because I wanted to have a classic vanilla-based cheesecake, and then have the chocolate chips throughout, as well as a swirl of chocolate spread. They are heavenly.

MAKES: 15

PREP: 30 minutes
BAKE: 40 minutes
COOL: 1 hour
SET: 6+ hours
DECORATE: 15 minutes
LASTS: 3+ days,
in the fridge

300g digestive biscuits
25g cocoa powder
125g unsalted butter, melted

Filling

500g full-fat soft cheese
3 eggs
75g soft light brown sugar
75g caster sugar
50g soured cream or natural
   yoghurt
1 tsp vanilla extract
100g chocolate chips of choice
100g chocolate spread, melted

Preheat the oven to 200°C/180°C fan and line a 23cm (9in) square baking tray with parchment paper.

Blitz the biscuits to a fine crumb in a food processor or crush in a bowl with a rolling pin.

Add the cocoa powder and mix, then stir through the melted butter.

Press the base into the bottom of the lined tin and bake in the oven for 10 minutes.

Filling

Reduce the oven temperature to 180°C/160°C fan.

Add the soft cheese to a large bowl and mix to loosen it. Add the eggs and both sugars and continue to mix until smooth. Stir through the soured cream or natural yoghurt and vanilla extract and then fold through the chocolate chips. Pour onto the base and then swirl through the melted chocolate spread. Bake in the oven for 30 minutes. Turn off the oven and leave the cheesecake to cool in the oven with the door slightly ajar for 1 hour.

Place the tray in the fridge and set overnight.

NOTES

- *You can use other flavours, such as 1 teaspoon of lemon, orange or almond extract, then swap the chocolate chips to match (I'd use white chocolate with lemon extract).*

- *You can remove the cocoa powder for a plain biscuit base.*

NO-BAKE RASPBERRY TART

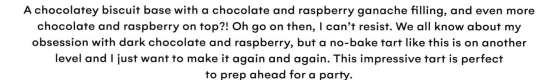

A chocolatey biscuit base with a chocolate and raspberry ganache filling, and even more chocolate and raspberry on top?! Oh go on then, I can't resist. We all know about my obsession with dark chocolate and raspberry, but a no-bake tart like this is on another level and I just want to make it again and again. This impressive tart is perfect to prep ahead for a party.

SERVES: 12

PREP: 30 minutes
COOK: 10 minutes
SET: 5 hours
DECORATE: 10 minutes
LASTS: 3+ days,
in the fridge

300g digestive biscuits
25g cocoa powder
125g unsalted butter, melted

Filling

100g raspberry jam
150g raspberries
150ml double cream
225g dark chocolate
35g unsalted butter

Decoration

Raspberries
Chocolate shavings

Blitz the biscuits to a fine crumb in a food processor or crush in a bowl with a rolling pin.

Mix through the cocoa powder. Add the melted butter and mix together. Press into the sides and base of a loose-bottomed 23cm tart tin. Chill for 15 minutes.

Filling

Spread the raspberry jam carefully over the base and sprinkle on the raspberries.

Add the double cream to a pan and heat until just before boiling point.

In a separate bowl, add the dark chocolate and butter, then pour over the hot cream. Whisk together until smooth. If the chocolate is still not completely melted, heat for 10-second bursts in the microwave until smooth. Pour the chocolate mixture onto the base and refrigerate for 1 hour.

Decoration

Decorate with raspberries and chocolate shavings, then chill again for another 3–4 hours. Remove from the tin.

NOTES

- *The raspberries and jam can be swapped for other flavours such as strawberry or cherry.*

- *For a plain biscuit base, omit the cocoa powder.*

- *If you want a lighter chocolate filling, use 150g dark chocolate and 150g milk chocolate instead of the 250g dark chocolate.*

CORNFLAKE TART

Another blast from the past, and one of my favourite bakes ever. I have had endless requests for a cornflake tart because it's so iconic and easy... so here you go! A homemade sweet shortcrust pastry with a jam filling, topped with a super-simple cornflake crust. It's the balance of sweetness, texture and nostalgia in this bake that does it for me, and I can't keep up with the requests for making it again and again! Of course, you can use whichever flavour jam you prefer, but raspberry is my favourite for this bake.

SERVES: 12–15+

PREP: 30 minutes
BAKE: 30 minutes
COOL: 1 hour
LASTS: 3+ days,
in the fridge

175g plain flour, plus extra for
dusting
100g chilled unsalted butter,
cubed, plus extra for greasing
1 tbsp icing sugar
1 egg yolk
Cold water

Filling

150g golden syrup
50g unsalted butter
35g soft light brown sugar
125g cornflakes
150g jam of choice (I use
raspberry)

Add the flour, cubed butter and icing sugar to a bowl and rub together with your fingertips until the mixture resembles breadcrumbs. Add the egg yolk and add 1 teaspoon of water at a time to help the dough come together, but try to use as little water as possible.

Grease and flour a 23cm (9in) tart tin.

Roll out the pastry onto a lightly floured work surface to the thickness of a £1 coin (3mm/⅛in). Carefully press the pastry into the prepared tart tin, making sure to press into the sides very well. I do not cut off the overhang of pastry. Chill the pastry case in the fridge while the oven preheats to 200°C/180°C fan.

Once the oven is at temperature, line the pastry case with parchment paper and fill with baking beans or uncooked rice. Bake in the oven for 15 minutes, then remove the parchment paper and beans/rice and bake for a further 5 minutes. Leave to cool for 10 minutes, then trim off the excess pastry with a sharp knife to create the perfect pastry case.

Filling

Heat the syrup, butter and sugar in a pan until smooth. Mix through the cornflakes.

Spread the jam onto the pastry case, then top with the cornflake mixture. Spread and gently press down. Return the tart to the oven and bake for 10 minutes. Leave to cool and enjoy.

NOTES

- Use whatever flavour jam you want.

- If you're short on time, you can use 1 sheet of shop-bought shortcrust pastry.

MANGO PASSION FRUIT TART

Mango is one of my favourite fruits, and I regularly just snack on an entire mango if I have the chance. I adore the flavour and adding it into a dessert is even better. I've shared a few mango recipes before, but this one is just stunning. I use a no-bake biscuit base here, but it would work wonderfully with a baked pastry base as well. The sweetened mascarpone cream filling is light and delicate and mixed with the fruity flavours of passion fruit and mango, it's incredible and very moreish. Take it to the next level with the decoration if you fancy – I think even more fruit on top finishes it off perfectly.

SERVES: 10

PREP: 30 minutes
SET: 4+ hours
DECORATE: 20 minutes
LASTS: 3+ days,
in the fridge

300g digestive biscuits
125g unsalted butter, melted

Filling

200ml double cream
150g mascarpone
50g icing sugar
75g mango purée
4 passion fruit

Decoration

1–2 ripe mangoes
150ml double cream
2 tbsp icing sugar
Zest of 1 lime
1–2 passion fruit

Blitz the biscuits to a fine crumb in a food processor or crush in a bowl with a rolling pin.

Add the melted butter and mix together until it resembles wet sand in texture. Press into the sides and base of a 23cm (9in) loose-bottomed tart tin.

Filling

In a large bowl, whisk the double cream, mascarpone and icing sugar together until smooth and starting to thicken. Fold through the mango purée and passion fruit pulp. Pour onto the biscuit base and put in the fridge for at least 4 hours.

Decoration

Slice the mangoes thinly and arrange around the edges of the tart. Whip the double cream lightly with the icing sugar and dollop into the middle. Sprinkle over the lime zest and add some extra passion fruit pulp.

NOTES

- *Leave out the decoration if you prefer.*

- *If you struggle to find mango purée, check the baby food section as there are often small pouches there.*

CHOCOLATE ORANGE COOKIE DOUGH DESSERTS

Well, let's just start this by saying that I LOVE COOKIES. Honestly, they are probably one of my favourite treats, potentially beating cheesecakes. I know, that's a bit of a shocker, but I don't think I have ever met someone who doesn't enjoy a cookie every now and again. One of the good things about cookies is that you can get a classic cookie, or cookie bars, or indulgently epic desserts such as this one. Hello, my idea of heaven in every single bite. Gooey, delicious, chocolate orange cookie dough served with ice cream and oodles of chocolate. Triple chocolate in this case. (Insert the dribbling emoji here because it is NEEDED.)

SERVES: 2

PREP: 5 minutes
BAKE: 12–15 minutes
COOL: 5 minutes
LASTS: 3+ days, at room temperature (but best served fresh)

60g unsalted butter or baking spread
100g soft light brown sugar
1 egg
Zest of 1 orange
½ tsp vanilla extract
100g plain flour
25g cocoa powder
½ tsp bicarbonate of soda
150g white, milk and dark chocolate chips
2–4 tbsp chocolate spread
Ice cream, to serve

Preheat the oven to 180°C/160°C fan and grab two crème brûlée dishes or ramekins (mine are about 12cm/4½in wide).

Melt the butter in a pan or in a heatproof bowl in the microwave. (If you've melted the butter in a pan, pour it into a bowl.) Add the sugar and mix together. Add the egg, orange zest and vanilla extract and mix again.

Add the flour, cocoa powder, bicarbonate of soda and chocolate chips and mix until combined. Add half of the cookie dough to the pots, spoon over some chocolate spread, then top with the remaining cookie dough.

Bake in the oven for 12–15 minutes, or until baked. Leave to cool for 5 minutes and serve with ice cream.

NOTES

- These can be made plain by replacing the cocoa powder with plain flour.

- Use some chopped chocolate orange if you want even more chocolate orange flavour.

AIR FRY

- Cook at 160°C for 10–12 minutes.

APPLE PIE

I like baking classic dishes, so finally sharing my apple pie recipe with you all is EXCITING.
I wanted to make this recipe as easy as possible and, honestly, it really is. I use a homemade
pastry with a little sweetness, but you can use a shop-bought shortcrust pastry if you want,
no judgement here. It may sound weird to slice the apples, pat them dry, then coat them in
flour, sugar and cinnamon, but trust the process. You can get fancy with the decoration,
but crimping the pastry shut with a fork is all you really need.

SERVES: 8

PREP: 45 minutes
CHILL: 1 hour
BAKE: 35–40 minutes
COOL: 10 minutes
LASTS: Best served fresh

350g plain flour, plus extra
  for dusting
200g chilled unsalted butter,
  cubed
25g caster sugar
1 egg
Cold water
Beaten egg or milk, for glazing

Filling

1kg Bramley apples
125g soft light brown sugar,
  plus extra for sprinkling
½ tbsp ground cinnamon
50g plain flour

Add the flour, cubed butter and sugar to a bowl and rub together
with your fingertips until the mixture resembles breadcrumbs. Add
the egg and water, 1 teaspoon at a time, and mix in with your hand,
then knead well until the dough comes together. Wrap in clingfilm
and chill for 1 hour.

Filling

Peel and core the apples, then thinly slice them about 5mm (¼in)
thick. Lay the slices onto sheets of parchment paper, top with
kitchen paper and leave to sit while the pastry chills.

Preheat the oven to 200°C/180°C fan.

On a floured work surface, roll out two-thirds of the dough into a
large circle and press into the base and sides of a 23cm (9in) pie
dish, making sure to leave a slight overhang.

Pat the apples dry, then tip into a bowl with the sugar, cinnamon
and flour and mix together. Pour into the pie dish and press them
down and even them out.

Roll out the remaining third of the pastry into a circle and use it to
top the pie dish. Use a fork or similar to seal the two bits of pastry
together and use a knife to trim off any excess. Cut a little cross in
the middle for steam to escape. Brush the top with egg wash or milk,
and sprinkle on some extra sugar.

Bake for 35–40 minutes until golden. Leave to sit for 10 minutes.

NOTES

- *I love serving my apple pie with whipped cream, custard or ice cream.*

- *I use Bramley or cooking apples as they create the perfect texture after
  baking. If you use eating apples, they may become mushy.*

BERRY CRUMBLE POTS

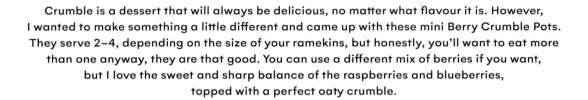

Crumble is a dessert that will always be delicious, no matter what flavour it is. However, I wanted to make something a little different and came up with these mini Berry Crumble Pots. They serve 2–4, depending on the size of your ramekins, but honestly, you'll want to eat more than one anyway, they are that good. You can use a different mix of berries if you want, but I love the sweet and sharp balance of the raspberries and blueberries, topped with a perfect oaty crumble.

SERVES: 2–4

PREP: 15 minutes
BAKE: 25–30 minutes
LASTS: Best served fresh

150g raspberries
100g blueberries
1 tbsp water
25g caster sugar
Vanilla ice cream, to serve

Crumble

30g plain flour
30g rolled oats
30g light brown sugar
30g unsalted butter

Preheat the oven to 180°C/160°C fan and grab 2–4 ramekins.

Add the raspberries, blueberries, water and sugar to a bowl and mix. Divide the mixture between the ramekins.

Crumble

Add the flour, oats, sugar and butter to a bowl and rub together with your fingertips until the mixture resembles breadcrumbs. Scatter over the fruit mixture in the ramekins.

Bake in the oven for 25–30 minutes. Top with a scoop of vanilla ice cream and enjoy.

NOTES

- *Any berries can be used, I just use what I have in the fridge.*

- *You can use shop-bought crumble mix if you prefer but it's super easy to make yourself.*

AIR FRY

- *Cook at 180°C for 13–16 minutes.*

SPECULOOS APPLE CRUMBLE

As with my Berry Crumble Pots recipe on page 140, I'm taking crumble up a notch here. This time, it's speculoos-themed. Apple and speculoos are the ideal match, so much so that I often just dunk apple chunks in the spread, but when you combine speculoos biscuits and spread in a classic apple crumble, you get something out of this world. I dollop a load of the spread over the apple mixture, then crumble the biscuits into the topping too. Serve with ice cream, custard or cream… and even extra speculoos spread.

SERVES: 6–8+

PREP: 30 minutes
BAKE: 40–45 minutes
LASTS: Best served fresh

750g Bramley apples
25g plain flour
1 tsp ground cinnamon
75g soft light brown sugar
200g speculoos spread (I use Biscoff), plus extra to serve (optional)
Ice cream, cream or custard, to serve

Crumble

150g plain flour
75g soft light brown sugar
75g unsalted butter
75g speculoos biscuits (I use Biscoff), crushed

Peel and chop the apples into 2.5cm (1in) cubes. Add the apples to a large bowl with the flour, cinnamon and sugar and stir together.

Crumble

Add the flour, sugar and butter to a bowl and rub together with your fingertips until the mixture resembles breadcrumbs. Mix through the crushed biscuits.

Preheat the oven to 200°C/180°C fan and grab a medium baking dish.

Pour the apple mixture into the dish and then dollop over the speculoos spread. Sprinkle over the crumble mixture. Bake in the oven for 40–45 minutes until golden and delicious.

Serve immediately with ice cream, cream or custard (with an extra speculoos drizzle, if you fancy).

NOTES

- *You can use the smooth or crunchy speculoos spread.*

- *If you use eating apples instead of cooking apples, they may become softer and mushier.*

NO-BAKE MICROWAVE LEMON PUDDING

I love a quick pudding because sometimes you forget to prepare one in advance, or you suddenly want something to satisfy a sweet craving NOW. A microwave pudding is a quick way to solve this problem, and it's just SO easy! It has a classic cake base but microwaved in a small dish for four people, and it works wonderfully. This perfect warm pudding can be served with custard, or even ice cream... or just the entire dish with a spoon! You can switch up the flavour to orange or lime, or even swap 25g of flour for cocoa powder for a chocolatey pud instead.

SERVES: 4

PREP: 5 minutes
BAKE: 3 minutes
COOL: 10 minutes
LASTS: Best served fresh

125g unsalted butter, at room
    temperature
125g caster sugar
125g self-raising flour
2 eggs
Zest of 1 lemon
100g lemon curd
Custard, ice cream or whipped
    cream, to serve

In a bowl, cream the butter and sugar together. Add the flour, eggs and lemon zest and mix until well combined. Pour the batter into a heatproof dish about 20 x 15cm (8 x 6in) in size. Microwave on full power for 3 minutes. Timings may vary depending on the power of your microwave, so keep an eye on it while it cooks!

Pour over the lemon curd and spread. Cool for 10 minutes and serve with custard, ice cream or whipped cream.

NOTES

- *You can use 1 teaspoon of lemon extract instead of the lemon zest if you prefer.*

- *Top with other fruit curds if you fancy.*

- *Time in the microwave can vary, test with a skewer in intervals. The top may still look a little wet.*

PEACH COBBLER

Even though crumble is one of the best desserts, cobbler is just as good and I feel that it is really underrated and not talked about enough. I have a delicious peach crumble recipe on my blog, but I adore this cobbler topping. It's so easy to chuck together and bake and enjoy within the hour. The cobbler topping is a little richer and more cake-like than crumble, which is what you are looking for. I dollop mine on randomly, and it's ready to bake. You don't have to be precious about it, just whack it together and enjoy.

SERVES: 4

PREP: 20 minutes
BAKE: 35–40 minutes
LASTS: Best served fresh

2–3 x approx. 400g tins peach
  slices, drained
50g caster sugar
½ tsp ground ginger

Cobbler

150g plain flour
150g unsalted butter
100g caster sugar, plus extra
  for sprinkling
1 tsp baking powder
1 egg

Preheat the oven to 180°C/160°C fan and grab a medium baking dish.

Lay the peach slices on the base of the dish and sprinkle with the sugar and ginger.

Add the flour, butter, sugar and baking powder to a bowl and rub together with your fingertips until the mixture resembles breadcrumbs. Add the egg and use a spatula or your hands to bind the mixture together.

Dollop the cobbler mixture on top of the peaches, then sprinkle with a little extra sugar. Bake for 35–40 minutes until golden.

NOTES

- *I love to serve mine with ice cream.*

- *You can swap the peaches for other fruit, such as berries or pear.*

BANOFFEE TRIFLE

As we all know, I love a mash-up, but sometimes you just need a giant bowl of delicious ingredients, all layered up into a no-bake dessert. Just like this Banoffee Trifle. Layers of rum-soaked sponge, caramel, biscuits, bananas, custard and cream create a luxurious pudding guaranteed to make anyone happy. To make it super easy, I use shop-bought ingredients so this dessert can be thrown together in no time at all, but you can always make your own elements if you have the time.

SERVES: 10+

PREP: 30 minutes
ASSEMBLE: 30 minutes
SET: 2 hours
LASTS: 2+ days,
in the fridge (but
best served fresh)

600ml double cream
2 tbsp icing sugar
300g shop-bought Madeira
  sponge
200g digestive biscuits
50g unsalted butter, melted
6 bananas
3–4 tbsp spiced rum
397g tin caramel
500g shop-bought custard
Chocolate shavings

In a large bowl, whip the double cream with the icing sugar until soft peaks form. Cut the Madeira cake into 2.5cm (1in) thick slices.

Blitz the biscuits to a fine crumb in a food processor or crush in a bowl with a rolling pin. Add the melted butter and mix together.

Slice the bananas into 2.5cm (1in) thick slices.

Assemble the cake slices on the bottom of a trifle bowl, then drizzle over the rum. Pour over half the caramel and spread evenly. Add half the sliced bananas. Pour on the custard and spread until even. Add the biscuit mixture and press down slightly. Add the remaining caramel and spread, then add the rest of the bananas. Top with the whipped cream and decorate with chocolate shavings.

NOTES

- *For a child-friendly pudding, leave out the rum.*

- *You can swap the Madeira cake for Swiss roll.*

N

LEMON MERINGUE ICE CREAM

The wonderful thing about a no-churn ice cream is that you don't need to use anything fancy to make it! No ice-cream machine, no cooking a custard mixture first; nothing. The main idea of this recipe is the lemon flavour – some people may not want to include the meringue and just have a delicious lemon ice cream, and that is totally fine. You can use lemon extract, lemon zest and juice, or just use the lemon curd. I found using the lemon extract along with the curd gave the best results, because you don't risk the ice cream splitting, and the flavour comes through much stronger.

SERVES: 10

PREP: 20 minutes
FREEZE: 4+ hours
LASTS: 3 months,
in the freezer

600ml double cream
397g tin condensed milk
2 tsp lemon extract
300g lemon curd
6 meringue nests

In a large bowl, whisk the double cream, condensed milk and lemon extract together until it's starting to thicken.

Layer the ice cream mix, blobs of lemon curd and crumbled meringue into a 900g loaf tin (or any freezerproof container). Freeze for at least 4 hours until solid.

Remove from the freezer 10 minutes before serving to soften slightly.

NOTES

- *You can use any flavour curd if you want.*

PEACH SORBET

This sorbet uses just five ingredients to make one of the best desserts I have ever tasted, and that is saying something. Sugar, water, peach slices, golden syrup and a lemon come together in the BEST sorbet ever, and it's entirely homemade. I spent so long getting this recipe perfect, and to be honest I love it so much that sometimes it doesn't even make it to the freezer... I find it far easier to use frozen peach slices as I am too lazy to prep that many peaches, but obviously if it is peak peach season, then go for it!

SERVES: 6–8

PREP: 15 minutes
FREEZE: 1–2+ hours
LASTS: 3 months, in the freezer

175g granulated or caster sugar
175ml water
600g frozen peach slices
2 tbsp golden syrup
Zest and juice of 1 lemon

Add the sugar and water to a pan and heat over a high heat until the sugar has dissolved.

Add the peaches, syrup, lemon zest and juice and sugar syrup to a blender and blend until smooth. Transfer to a freezerproof container and freeze for at least 1–2 hours until solid. Remove from the freezer 5 minutes before serving.

NOTES

- *This will work with other fruits as well but some will have texture due to their seeds, such as raspberries.*

Sweet Treats

MINI BERRY PASTRIES

I wanted to create a five-ingredient sweet snack that's fun to make, and so light, fruity and full of flavour you'll want to make it again and again. I went for a slightly fancier pastry shape, but honestly, these are SO easy, yet look so elegant. A puff pastry base topped with mascarpone and berries creates the perfect snack, breakfast pastry or afternoon tea treat.

MAKES: 8

PREP: 30 minutes
CHILL: 1 hour
BAKE: 20–25 minutes
COOL: 30 minutes
LASTS: 2+ days,
in the fridge (but best
served fresh)

150g mixed berries (fresh
  or frozen)
3 tbsp icing sugar
1 tbsp plain flour, plus extra for
  dusting
1 x sheet of puff pastry
100g mascarpone

Add the berries to a pan with 2 tablespoons of the icing sugar and the flour and simmer for 5 minutes until the sugar is dissolved (7 minutes if the berries are frozen). Continue to simmer for a further 5 minutes to soften the fruit. Pour the mixture into a bowl and chill for about 1 hour.

Preheat the oven to 180°C/160°C fan and line two large baking trays with parchment paper.

On a floured work surface, roll out the pastry sheet and cut into 8 pieces. Cut a square out of the centre of each piece and thread one corner through the square to the other side, creating a diamond shape. Press down the pastry lightly to hold.

Mix the mascarpone with the remaining 1 tablespoon of icing sugar and dollop/spread in the middle of each piece of pastry. Top with the berry mixture.

Bake in the oven for 20–25 minutes, then leave to cool to room temperature.

NOTES

- *You can use any berries you fancy; I like using a ready-made mixture.*

AIR FRY

- *Cook at 180°C for 10–12 minutes.*

5

APPLE BITES

After finally giving you my delicious Apple Pie recipe on page 138, I wanted to give you another sweet treat of apple goodness because these are so fun to make, and easier to serve at a party or gathering. Five simple ingredients create a fun snack for everyone, with a delicious classic flavour. You can easily switch up how you style these by changing how you cut the apple and slice the pastry, but I went for one of the easier croissant-style bakes because they're super fun.

MAKES: 12

PREP: 10 minutes
BAKE: 20–25 minutes
COOL: 10 minutes
LASTS: 2–3 days,
in the fridge (but
best served fresh)

1 x sheet of puff pastry
2 eating apples, each sliced into
   6 pieces
25g unsalted butter, melted
Soft light brown sugar
Ground cinnamon

Preheat the oven to 190°C/170°C fan and line two baking trays with parchment paper.

Roll out the puff pastry into a square with a rolling pin and slice into 12 triangles. Grab a piece of apple and roll it up in the pastry like a croissant. Brush the top with melted butter, then sprinkle over a little sugar and cinnamon.

Bake in the oven for 20–25 minutes. Leave to cool slightly before enjoying.

NOTES

- *I love grabbing some caramel sauce and using it as a dip.*

- *For extra crunch, add a few chopped nuts with the apple if you wish.*

AIR FRY

- *Cook at 170°C for 10–12 minutes.*

5

ROCK CAKES

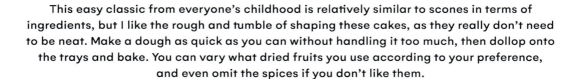

This easy classic from everyone's childhood is relatively similar to scones in terms of ingredients, but I like the rough and tumble of shaping these cakes, as they really don't need to be neat. Make a dough as quick as you can without handling it too much, then dollop onto the trays and bake. You can vary what dried fruits you use according to your preference, and even omit the spices if you don't like them.

MAKES: 10

PREP: 20 minutes
BAKE: 18–22 minutes
COOL: 30 minutes
LASTS: 2+ days, at room temperature (but best served fresh)

275g self-raising flour
75g caster sugar
1 tsp baking powder
½ tsp mixed spice
½ tsp ground cinnamon
½ tsp ground ginger
100g unsalted butter
1 egg
50ml whole milk
1 tsp vanilla extract
175g dried fruit

Preheat the oven to 180°C/160°C fan and line two large baking trays with parchment paper.

Add the flour, sugar, baking powder, mixed spice, cinnamon and ginger to a bowl. Add the butter and rub it in using your fingertips until the mixture resembles breadcrumbs. Add the egg, milk and vanilla extract and mix together. Towards the end of mixing, add the dried fruit and mix until it all just comes together. Using a tablespoon, dollop 10 cakes onto the lined trays.

Bake in the oven for 18–22 minutes until golden and baked through. Leave to cool fully and enjoy.

NOTES

- *Omit the spices if you prefer – these cakes are still delicious without.*

- *You can use all of one type of dried fruit, such as raisins, or you can use a mixed bag.*

BELGIAN BUNS

A sweetened bread is one of my favourite things to cook because I find making the dough so therapeutic, as well as enjoying the tasty treat you get at the end. Making bread dough is somewhat easier when you have a mixer with a dough hook, but it's also super simple to knead the dough together with your hands. The lemon and sultana filling is so good, and although this recipe takes a little longer, it's really easy to throw together. Do the second prove in the fridge overnight, bring it back to room temperature and bake in the morning for a breakfast treat!

MAKES: 6

PREP: 1 hour
PROVE: 2–3 hours
BAKE: 20–22 minutes
DECORATE: 10 minutes
COOL: 30 minutes
SET: 30–60 minutes
LASTS: 2+ days, at room temperature (but best served fresh)

300g strong white bread flour, plus extra for dusting
7g dried active yeast
35g caster sugar
45g chilled unsalted butter, cubed
125ml whole milk
1 tsp vanilla extract
1 egg yolk

Filling
100g lemon curd
100g sultanas

Decoration
100g icing sugar
Water
6 glacé cherries

Add the flour, yeast, sugar and butter to the bowl of a stand mixer fitted with the dough hook and rub together with your fingertips until the mixture resembles breadcrumbs.

Heat the milk in a pan or in the microwave until warm, then pour into the mixture, along with the vanilla extract and egg yolk. Knead this together for 7–10 minutes until the dough is smooth and elastic in the mixer. If you don't have a mixer, this can be done by hand with a little more time. Look out for a smooth and elastic texture. Transfer the dough to a lightly oiled bowl and cover with clingfilm. Leave to rise for 1–2 hours, or until doubled in size.

Filling
Transfer the dough to a lightly floured surface. Roll out the dough into a large rectangle.

Spread over the lemon curd, then sprinkle over the sultanas. Roll up the dough tightly into a long sausage from long side to long side.

Slice the dough into 6 buns and add into a medium baking dish (30 x 20cm/12 x 8in), spaced well apart from each other. Cover the buns with clingfilm and leave to rise again for about an hour, until they are just touching.

Towards the end of the proving, preheat the oven to 180°C/160°C fan.

Remove the clingfilm and bake the buns in the oven for 20–22 minutes, or until golden brown. Leave to cool.

Decoration
While the buns are cooling, add the icing sugar to a large bowl. Gradually add the water until you have a thick paste. Drizzle this over the buns. Add a glacé cherry per bun. Leave the icing to set for 30–60 minutes and then devour.

MICROWAVE BROWNIES

As with my No-Bake Microwave Lemon Pudding on page 144, I wanted to create a treat that is easy to throw together and ready in ten minutes. This thick brownie mixture is so gooey when it's fresh out of the microwave, and it's ideal to top with a bit of ice cream and devour. It technically serves four people, but I'm not judging if you want to have a bowl of this to yourself… It's perfect for movie night or to answer that sweet craving for you and your partner. In my opinion, the rich chocolatey goodness of a brownie cannot be beaten.

MAKES: 4–6

PREP: 5 minutes
BAKE: 3–5 minutes
COOL: 10 minutes
LASTS: 3+ days,
at room temperature

125g unsalted butter
200g soft light brown sugar
1 tsp vanilla extract
75g cocoa powder
75g plain flour
2 eggs
150g chocolate chips of choice

Add the butter to a heatproof bowl and microwave until melted. Add the sugar and vanilla extract and mix until combined. Add the cocoa powder, flour and eggs and mix again. Stir through the chocolate chips.

Pour into a 20 x 15cm (8 x 6in) heatproof dish. Microwave on full power for 3–5 minutes. Timings may vary depending on the power of your microwave, so keep an eye on it while it cooks!

Leave to cool for 10 minutes, then enjoy.

NOTES

- *You can use any flavour of chocolate chip you want.*

- *Try swirling through 50–75g of your favourite chocolate spread, nut butter or biscuit spread.*

- *Try serving warm with ice cream or a drizzle of double cream.*

CINNAMON KNOTS

These are a really fun twist (they are knots after all) on cinnamon rolls. This makes a smaller batch than most cinnamon roll recipes, making only 6–8 knots of a similar size (but you will want to devour at least three yourself). I tend to twist the strips of dough a few times, then lightly knot them, tucking the ends underneath. This is an incredibly easy recipe; however, you do need a little patience with the proving time, but honestly, these knots are worth the wait.

MAKES: 6–8

PREP: 1 hour
PROVE: 2–3 hours
BAKE: 20–25 minutes
COOL: 30 minutes
LASTS: 2+ days, at room temperature (but best served fresh)

250g plain flour
5g dried active yeast
35g caster sugar
35g unsalted butter
135ml whole milk
1 tsp vanilla extract
Icing sugar

Filling

25g unsalted butter, melted
75g soft light brown sugar
1 tbsp ground cinnamon

Add the flour, yeast, sugar and butter to a large bowl and rub together with your fingertips until the mixture resembles breadcrumbs.

Heat the milk in a pan or in the microwave until warm, then pour into the mixture with the vanilla and begin to knead the dough. After 7–8 minutes of kneading, when the dough is springy, transfer it to a lightly oiled bowl and cover with clingfilm. Leave to rise for 1–2 hours, or until doubled in size.

Shaping and Filling

Once the dough has doubled in size, place on a lightly floured surface and roll out into a 30 x 20cm (12 x 8in) rectangle. Brush the melted butter onto the dough, then sprinkle over the sugar and cinnamon. Fold one half of the dough onto the other (from short side to short side), then slice into 6–8 strips. Twist each strip a few times, then fold into a knot. Place the strips onto a lined baking tray, spaced apart from each other. Cover lightly with an oiled piece of clingfilm and leave for 30–45 minutes to rise again and double in size.

Baking

Towards the end of the proving process, preheat the oven to 180°C/160°C fan.

Bake in the oven for 20–25 minutes. Leave to cool for 30 minutes, then dust with icing sugar and enjoy.

NOTES

- *To change up the flavours, add the zest of 1 lemon or orange to the dough.*

- *You can also omit the cinnamon from the filling or switch it for a different spice such as ginger or cardamom.*

WAFFLES

~~~~

If I had to think of a sweet and delicious brunch or breakfast idea, I would think of waffles. Pancakes are also an option, but waffles are just on another level, although you will need a waffle maker to cook them. My easy waffle batter is so simple to whisk together in a bowl and then you can just cook the waffles as required. The choice of topping is entirely up to you, so use what you LOVE. I went for melted chocolate, berries and ice cream because they are peak-level perfection for me.

MAKES: 6

PREP: 15 minutes
BAKE: 10 minutes
LASTS: Best served fresh

175g self-raising flour
1 tsp baking powder
1 tbsp caster sugar
1 egg
250ml whole milk
1 tsp vanilla extract

To Serve

Melted chocolate
Fresh berries of choice
Ice cream

In a large bowl, whisk the flour, baking powder and sugar together. Add the egg, milk and vanilla extract and whisk to combine.

Turn on your waffle maker and heat fully. Ladle in the mixture and cook according to the manufacturer's instructions (timings will vary depending on the brand of your machine).

Serve with melted chocolate, berries and ice cream.

NOTES

- *To make chocolate waffles, substitute 20g of the flour for cocoa powder.*

- *If you don't have a waffle maker you can use a small 15cm frying pan or griddle pan and cook the batter in batches. This will make thinner waffles, almost like pancakes:*

- *Add a small amount of butter to a pan over a medium heat then add a ladle of batter and fry for 3-5 minutes on each side, until golden.*

30

BERRY BAKED OATS

This recipe is the perfect breakfast bake to prep in advance if you want something healthy and different for your morning nourishment, or it's also great as a healthier snack. It's designed for one, but you can easily multiply it to serve more people or prep more servings for yourself. You can use whatever sweetener you have in the cupboard, whether it's honey, golden syrup or maple syrup, and any berries that you also happen to have in your fridge or freezer.

SERVES: 1

PREP: 3 minutes
BAKE: 15–20 minutes
COOL: 5 minutes
LASTS: 1–2+ days, at room temperature
(but best served fresh)

50g rolled oats
1 medium banana
1 egg
1 tbsp honey or golden or maple syrup
½ tsp baking powder
½ tsp vanilla extract
50g berries of choice

Preheat the oven to 180°C/160°C fan and grab a small baking dish or larger ramekin.

Add the oats, banana, egg, honey or syrup, baking powder and vanilla to a blender and blend until smooth. Pour into the baking dish and sprinkle on the berries. Bake in the oven for 15–20 minutes. Leave to cool for 5 minutes and enjoy.

NOTES

- *You can add 10g cocoa powder if you want a chocolate flavour.*

- *Any berries can be used.*

- *Just multiply the quantities to serve more people.*

AIR FRY

- *Cook at 160°C for 10–15 minutes.*

BROWNIE BATTER DIP

When I think of my favourite treat when I was younger, it involved brownies and chocolate. If I could have anything chocolatey, I would. My ultimate treat was a brownie, dipped in chocolate. This made me want to make something that is slightly OTT, which is a chocolatey dip that tastes exactly like brownie batter, and wow it's incredible. The best way to describe this would be a chocolatey soft cheese frosting, but the little bit of brown sugar creates a depth that makes it taste like raw brownie mix. Dip away to your heart's content.

SERVES: 6+

PREP: 15 minutes
LASTS: 2+ days, in the fridge (but best served fresh)

125g unsalted butter, at room temperature
100g icing sugar
15g cocoa powder
25g soft light brown sugar
250g full-fat soft cheese
1 tsp vanilla extract
200g chocolate chips of choice

To Serve
Fruit, such as apple slices or strawberries
Biscuits
Brownie bites

In a large bowl, beat the butter for a few minutes to loosen it. Add the icing sugar, cocoa powder and light brown sugar and beat again until smooth. Add the soft cheese and vanilla extract and beat again until smooth. It may look lumpy at first but will smooth out eventually. Finally, fold through the chocolate chips.

Transfer the mixture into a new bowl and chill until required.

Serve with apple slices, strawberries, biscuits, brownie bites or anything else you prefer.

NOTES

- *I use dark chocolate as it balances the recipe well and makes it taste more brownie-like.*

- *Leave out the chocolate chips if you like.*

SPECULOOS FUDGE

We all know how much I adore speculoos, right?! And my readers and followers love it too. This popular recipe of mine has been made thousands and thousands of times already, because it really is SO easy and SO good. It's four simple ingredients and basically a bit of a cheat's fudge. Fudge classically uses more ingredients, including cream, sugar and even golden syrup, which means you need a thermometer to get it accurate. However, my recipe consists of chocolate and condensed milk, then you mix in the speculoos spread, add some biscuits for crunch and set... It really is that simple.

MAKES: 25

PREP: 10 minutes
SET: 3–4 hours
LASTS: 7+ days,
in the fridge

397g tin condensed milk
500g white chocolate
125g speculoos spread
(I use Biscoff)
125g speculoos biscuits
(I use Biscoff)

Line a 23cm (9in) square tin with parchment paper.

Add the condensed milk and white chocolate to a large heatproof bowl. Melt on a low heat in the microwave, stirring well, until smooth. Alternatively, add to a large pan and melt together over a low heat. Add the speculoos spread and stir to combine. Fold through the speculoos biscuits.

Pour into the lined tin and spread out into an even layer. Set in the fridge for 3–4 hours.

NOTES

- *You can use smooth or crunchy speculoos spread.*

- *Swap the white chocolate for 450g milk chocolate, or substitute 400g dark chocolate instead.*

- *Leave out the biscuits if you like.*

- *You can use other biscuits or chocolate spreads if you prefer.*

SLOW COOKER

- *To make in a slow cooker, add all the ingredients to the slow cooker and cook on low for about 2 hours, stirring every 15 minutes or so. Pour into your tin to set as above*

5 N

CARAMEL COFFEE FUDGE

I am the classic coffee addict in the morning and feel like I can't function without a cup, but now I also feel like this applies to coffee-flavoured bakes... This recipe consists of caramel made from condensed milk, white chocolate and coffee. You can use all types of coffee, but for ease I use dissolved instant coffee as most people have access to it. You can increase or decrease how much you use to your taste. I decorate with a few chocolate-coated coffee beans, but these can sometimes be hard to find, so they are optional. You can substitute them for something else, such as chocolate chips, or leave them out entirely.

MAKES: 25

PREP: 10 minutes
SET: 3–4 hours
LASTS: 7+ days,
in the fridge

397g tin condensed milk caramel
600g white chocolate
2 tbsp instant coffee, dissolved in
    1–2 tbsp boiling water
Chocolate-covered coffee beans
    (optional)

Line a 23cm (9in) square tin with parchment paper.

Add the condensed milk caramel and white chocolate to a large heatproof bowl. Melt on a low heat in the microwave, stirring well, until smooth. Alternatively, add to a large pan and melt together over a low heat. Add the coffee and stir to combine.

Pour into the lined tin and spread out evenly. Sprinkle over a few chocolate-covered coffee beans if you fancy. Set in the fridge for 3–4 hours.

NOTES

- *Try using 500g milk chocolate if you want or even 400g dark chocolate.*

- *If you just want coffee fudge, use regular condensed milk.*

- *You can switch the fresh coffee for 1–2 teaspoons of coffee extract or flavouring.*

SLOW COOKER

- *To make in a slow cooker, add all the ingredients to the slow cooker and cook on low for about 2 hours, stirring every 15 minutes or so. Pour into your tin to set as above.*

BROWNIE TRUFFLES

Even though people may not believe me, sometimes leftover brownies are a thing. If you have made enough for a party and there are a few leftovers, or you happen to find yourself a little bored of the classic brownie, these are what you should make. Pretty much any brownie can work, but I use homemade ones. The good thing about brownies being denser is that you can just mix them into a paste and roll them into balls to create the truffles. Decorate however you fancy, leave to set and enjoy a luxurious treat!

MAKES: 25–30

PREP: 10 minutes
SET: 30 minutes
DECORATE: 1 hour
LASTS: 7+ days,
in the fridge

500g brownies
250g milk chocolate
35g white chocolate

Add the brownies to a bowl and mix until they form a paste.

Using a 2-teaspoon scoop, spoon truffles onto a lined baking tray, then roll into balls. Freeze for 30 minutes.

In two separate heatproof bowls, break up the chocolate into pieces. Melt in the microwave in short bursts or set the bowls over a pan of simmering water (bain-marie) until smooth. Dunk each truffle into the melted milk chocolate. Drizzle over the melted white chocolate and leave to set.

NOTES

- *You can make a batch of brownies for the base using my Mint Chocolate Brownies recipe on page 86 without the peppermint extract.*

- *Use shop-bought brownies to save time, or if you don't have any leftovers.*

- *This recipe is based on half a batch of my brownies, so reduce the ratio depending on how many brownies you have.*

COOKIES AND CREAM TRUFFLES

Using soft cheese and biscuit crumbs is one of my favourite ways to make truffles, as it's so simple and so much easier than making a ganache. You just have to blend the biscuits to a fine crumb and mix in the soft cheese. It forms a paste, which is thick and a little sticky, but honestly, it's what you need. Portion the paste into truffles, then roll and freeze. Coat them in your favourite melted chocolate; I used milk chocolate for these, then added some extra biscuit crumbs because it's a simple and easy way to decorate them.

MAKES: 20–25

PREP: 30 minutes
CHILL: 30 minutes
SET: 1 hour, 30 minutes
DECORATE: 30 minutes
LASTS: 4–5+ days,
in the fridge

300g cookies and cream biscuits
   (I use Oreos)
125g full-fat soft cheese
250g milk chocolate

Blitz the biscuits to a fine crumb in a food processor or crush in a bowl with a rolling pin.

Reserve 1 tablespoon of biscuit crumbs and set aside.

Add the soft cheese to the rest of the biscuit crumbs and mix to form a thick paste. Using a melon baller or two teaspoons, portion the truffles and roll each one into a ball.

Place the truffles on a lined baking tray or plate and freeze for 30 minutes.

Once the truffles have chilled, break the chocolate into pieces in a heatproof bowl. Melt in the microwave in short bursts or set the bowl over a pan of simmering water (bain-marie) until smooth. Carefully dunk each truffle into the melted chocolate to coat, then place onto a clean lined tray. Sprinkle on the reserved biscuit crumbs.

Chill the truffles for 1 hour or so to finish setting, then enjoy.

NOTES

- *This recipe works with other biscuits, such as speculoos or bourbon biscuits.*

- *You can coat the truffles in whatever chocolate you want.*

PEANUT BRITTLE

Peanut brittle is a simple recipe that needs only three ingredients. I used peanut because it is one of the most famous nut brittles, but you can use any nut you prefer. This is a sweet, salty and crunchy treat that is good for decorating cakes, as a snack, or even as a gift. Making caramel might sound scary, but it isn't at all... Just ensure that you don't stir it, and keep it dead centre on the hob so the pan heats evenly, and it will simply melt away.

SERVES: 6+

PREP: 10 minutes
BAKE: 5–8 minutes
SET: 45 minutes
LASTS: 1+ week,
at room temperature

150g caster sugar
100g roasted peanuts
Sea salt (optional)

Line a large baking tray with parchment paper.

Add the sugar to a medium frying pan and heat over a medium heat for 5–8 minutes, without stirring. The sugar will begin to melt to a darker amber colour – if you need to move the sugar about, carefully tip the pan to adjust it but do not stir it.

Once all the sugar has melted to the dark amber colour, quickly pour in the peanuts, stir briefly and tip onto the lined tray. Sprinkle with sea salt, if you wish, and leave to set.

NOTES

- *Any nut can be used, or even a combination such as hazelnuts, pecans and walnuts.*

FRUIT AND NUT CHOCOLATE BARK

We all know that I adore chocolate bark, because how can you not?! Melt a load of chocolate, then decorate it however you like. This time I wanted to make a nutty chocolate bark because, like my Peanut Brittle on page 186, it's an easy homemade gift idea, a delicious, sweet snack and it's such a versatile recipe that you can cater to what or who you want! Use your favourite chocolate, or a combination of your faves, then whatever nuts you like, or a combination… you do you!

SERVES: 6+

PREP: 10 minutes
BAKE: 5 minutes
SET: 1 hour
LASTS: 1+ week,
at room temperature

400g chocolate (I use dark)
200g chopped nuts (I use pistachios and pecans)
200g dried fruit (I use raisins and sultanas)
1–2 tsp sea salt

In a heatproof bowl, break up the chocolate into pieces. Melt in the microwave in short bursts or set the bowl over a pan of simmering water (bain-marie) until smooth. Pour in most of the nuts and dried fruit, then stir.

Pour onto a large, lined baking tray and spread evenly. Sprinkle on the rest of the chopped nuts and fruit, then scatter over the sea salt and set in the fridge for 1 hour.

Break up and enjoy.

NOTES

- *You can use any nut, and any dried fruit.*

- *Leave out the salt if you prefer, but it adds a nice element of flavour and crunch.*

Savoury Meals

CHEESE AND ONION TART

Put homemade pastry, onion, so much cheese and a simple creamy filling together and you get a luxurious yet easy-to-make tart that is perfect for so many occasions. A lunchtime treat, a picnic, a dinner... whatever you want! You can always cheat and use shop-bought shortcrust pastry if you don't have time to make your own, but the recipe is super simple. I fry off my onion to soften it before pouring it over the pastry base, then tip over all the crumbled cheese. I use Stilton, Brie and Cheddar, but you can change the cheeses to your preference – I have also used Wensleydale and Cheddar, and added 125g fried bacon lardons for variation.

SERVES: 12

PREP: 90 minutes
COOK: 50–55 minutes
CHILL: 15 minutes
LASTS: 3+ days,
in the fridge

175g plain flour, plus extra for
  dusting
100g chilled unsalted butter,
  cubed, plus extra for greasing
½ tsp sea salt
1 egg yolk

Filling

1 tbsp butter
2 medium onions, thinly sliced
2 eggs
300ml double cream
Salt and pepper
100g Stilton, crumbled
100g Brie, cubed
100g Cheddar cheese, cubed

Add the flour, cubed butter and salt to a bowl and rub together with your fingertips until the mixture resembles breadcrumbs. Add the egg yolk and mix well with your hands, kneading until the dough comes together.

Grease and flour a 23cm (9in) tart tin.

Roll out the pastry on a lightly floured work surface to the thickness of a £1 coin (3mm/⅛in). Carefully press the pastry into the prepared tart tin, making sure to press into the sides. I do not cut off the overhang of pastry. Chill the pastry case in the fridge while the oven preheats to 200°C/180°C fan.

Once the oven is at temperature, line the pastry case with parchment paper and fill with baking beans or uncooked rice. Bake in the oven for 15 minutes, then remove the parchment paper and beans/rice and bake for a further 5 minutes.

Once baked, let it cool for 10 minutes, then trim off the excess pastry with a sharp knife to create the perfect pastry case.

Filling

While the pastry is baking, grab a medium pan and melt the butter over a medium-high heat. Fry the onions until softened.

In a bowl, whisk together the eggs and cream and season with salt and pepper.

Scatter the fried onions over the base of the tart case, sprinkle the cheese over the onions, then pour over the egg/cream mixture.

Reduce the oven temperature to 180°C/160°C fan and bake the tart in the oven for 30–35 minutes. Leave to cool slightly and then remove from the tin and enjoy.

CHEESY HAM AND LEEK BAKE

I love cheese, okay? I can't help myself – if I can add cheese, I will. A dish like this is so simple yet SO warming and cosy in every bite. Some recipes spend time wrapping bits of leek in ham, but I don't feel the need. Making a rich roux using butter and flour, then adding milk and white wine brings it up a notch. I flavour the sauce with mustard and thyme, which is perfect to pour over the ham and leeks, then top with Cheddar and Brie. Bake until it's golden, bubbling and fragrant. I dunk some of my homemade Crusty Bread (page 240) and serve with a salad for an easy weeknight dinner idea.

SERVES: 4+

PREP: 15 minutes
COOK: 30–35 minutes
LASTS: Best served fresh

500g leeks, sliced into 1cm (½in)
  thick pieces
200g ham, sliced into strips
50g unsalted butter
50g plain flour
300ml whole milk
175ml white wine
1 tsp wholegrain mustard
½ tsp dried thyme
Salt and pepper
100g Cheddar cheese, grated
100g Brie, cut into chunks

Preheat the oven to 210°C/190°C fan and grab a 1.5-litre ovenproof dish. Tip the sliced leeks and ham into the dish.

Add the butter to a medium pan and heat over a medium heat until melted. Add the flour and mix to combine. Cook out the flour over a medium heat for a couple of minutes, stirring well, then gradually start adding the milk. Mix well, then pour in the wine. Add the mustard, thyme and some salt and pepper to the sauce and simmer, stirring well, until thickened.

Pour the sauce over the leeks and ham, then mix slightly. Top with grated Cheddar and chunks of Brie and bake in the oven for 30–35 minutes until golden and bubbling.

NOTES

- Serve with chunks of bread and salad, or whatever you prefer.

- You can swap the cheese to whatever you like most; I just love the combination of Cheddar and Brie.

- Throw in whatever meat you have to hand – try chunks of cooked chicken or even bacon.

ONE-PAN PESTO CHICKEN

I love making a dish that just involves shoving everything into one pan and cooking, and this dish is exactly that. I wanted to create a recipe that was super simple but still had a nice punch. I tend to use chicken thighs because I prefer the flavour, but chicken breast chunks work as well. Cooking these slightly to start to brown them off, then mixing in the sun-dried tomatoes, asparagus, cherry tomatoes, green beans and pesto is so, so easy. Roast it all in one dish, then serve however you want – just as it is or with a salad alongside (or even my Potato Salad from page 258).

SERVES: 4

PREP: 10 minutes
BAKE: 45+ minutes
LASTS: Best served fresh

8–12 skinless, boneless chicken thighs
2 tbsp olive oil
Salt and pepper
100g sun-dried tomatoes
250g asparagus spears
200g cherry tomatoes
150g green beans
75g green or red pesto

Preheat the oven to 220°C/200°C fan and grab a large pan.

Add the chicken thighs to the pan, drizzle with the oil, then season with salt and pepper. Cook in the oven for 15 minutes, turning halfway through.

Once the 15 minutes is up, add the sun-dried tomatoes, asparagus spears, cherry tomatoes, green beans and pesto and toss together.

Bake for 15 minutes, check and stir, then bake for another 15 minutes. Serve immediately with salad or potatoes.

NOTES

- *You can use mini chicken fillets if you prefer those to thighs.*

AIR FRY

- *Cook at 180°C for 15 minutes. Turn the chicken, then add the pesto and veggies and cook for a further 10 minutes.*

SAUSAGE TRAYBAKE

Ever since this recipe went onto my blog it's been a success and I can see why. It's probably one of the simplest dishes you can make where you do actually put all the ingredients into one tray and cook. I use a mixture of onions, carrots and peppers, along with some new potatoes for the veg. You can use your favourite sausages, but if you use chipolatas, you'll want to add them halfway through as the cooking time is less. You can adapt the veg to whatever you fancy, or even just what you have in the fridge. Flavour it with a drizzle of honey, garlic, thyme and enjoy the perfect easy weeknight dinner.

SERVES: 4+

PREP: 10 minutes
BAKE: 40 minutes
LASTS: Best served fresh

2 onions, cut into 2.5cm (1in) chunks

2 carrots, cut into 2.5cm (1in) chunks

2 peppers, cut into 2.5cm (1in) chunks

200g new potatoes, halved

500g sausages of choice

1–2 tbsp olive oil

50g honey

2 tsp dried thyme

2 garlic cloves, sliced

Salt and pepper

Preheat the oven to 210°C/190°C fan and grab a large ovenproof baking dish.

Add the chopped onions, carrots, peppers, new potatoes and sausages to the dish. Drizzle over the olive oil and honey, then sprinkle over the dried thyme and garlic. Season with salt and pepper and toss everything together so it is well coated.

Bake in the oven for 20 minutes, then toss again and bake for another 20 minutes.

Serve immediately.

NOTES

- *I serve my sausage traybake with gravy, and you can add mash or another side if you wish.*

- *I use regular-sized sausages.*

- *You can cut the sausages into chunks as well.*

- *If you're vegetarian, just swap the meat sausages for veggie ones.*

AIR FRY

- *Cook at 180°C for 20 minutes, then turn and mix. Continue cooking, checking every 5 minutes until the sausages and veggies are cooked.*

CAJUN-STYLE SALMON

I am a big fan of a simple dish that involves a creamy sauce, plus meat or fish. Salmon is one of my favourite types of fish as it's hard to get it wrong, and it tastes so good. Some salmon fillets can be long and skinny and they do work, but they're hard to flip without breaking apart, so I prefer chunky, shorter pieces. Once the salmon is nearly cooked, take it out of the pan and whack in the garlic, then the spices and cream, thicken and season and you have a wonderfully rich, thick sauce. I serve mine with new potatoes, salad, or veggies – all ready in less than 30 minutes!

SERVES: 4

PREP: 10 minutes
COOK: 10–15 minutes
LASTS: Best served fresh

4 salmon fillets, skin on
1 tbsp olive oil
2 tbsp Cajun seasoning
Salt and pepper

Sauce

3 garlic cloves, finely chopped
1 tsp chilli flakes
½ tsp dried parsley
½ tsp dried thyme
½ tsp dried rosemary
225ml double cream
Salt and pepper
Juice of 1 lemon

Pat the salmon fillets dry with kitchen paper and then drizzle with the oil. Sprinkle on the Cajun seasoning, then season with salt and pepper.

Add the salmon, skin-side down, to a large pan over a medium-high heat. Cook for 2–3 minutes, then carefully turn over and repeat. Remove the salmon from the pan and set aside.

Sauce

Add the garlic cloves to the pan and start to cook. Add the chilli flakes, parsley, thyme and rosemary and fry for a minute or two. Pour in the double cream and mix together. Season with salt and pepper, then pour in the lemon juice and stir to combine.

Add the salmon back into the pan and simmer for a couple of minutes before serving.

NOTES

- *I like to serve my creamy Cajun salmon with new potatoes and salad, but you can serve it however you like.*

HONEY GARLIC CHICKEN

Honey, garlic and chicken, oh wow. I like chicken thighs here, but chicken breast works wonderfully well, too. I use cornflour to coat my chicken, then fry it off in the pan until golden while mixing together the sauce. Fry the garlic, then you just need to add the vinegar, soy, honey, salt and pepper to a jug and pour it into the pan and make it lovely, thick and sticky. This is one of my favourite recipes to make for friends and family, and serving it with sticky rice, tenderstem broccoli and even some chopped spring onions makes such a classy dish, that's super quick to make and very popular.

SERVES: 4+

PREP: 20 minutes
COOK: 20–30 minutes
LASTS: Best served fresh

600g skinless, boneless chicken
  thighs
50g cornflour
50g unsalted butter
2 tbsp white wine vinegar
1 tbsp dark soy sauce
100g honey
Salt and pepper
3–4 garlic cloves, finely chopped

Cut the chicken thighs into 4–6 chunks per thigh, then tip into a bowl with the cornflour. Toss the chicken pieces in the cornflour until coated.

Add half the butter to a large pan and heat over a medium-high heat. Add the chicken pieces to the pan and fry for a couple of minutes on each side until golden.

While the chicken is frying, add the white wine vinegar, soy sauce and honey to a bowl and mix to combine.

Season the chicken once it's nearly cooked and add the garlic to the pan with the remaining butter. Fry the garlic for a few minutes, then pour in the honey sauce and season with salt and pepper.

Toss the chicken in the sauce until each piece is coated and cook until the sauce has thickened, the chicken is cooked and it's nice and sticky. Serve immediately.

NOTES

- *I serve mine with some sticky rice, broccoli and some chopped spring onions.*

- *The chicken thighs can be substituted for chicken breast chunks, or even chicken wings if you prefer. The cooking time of the chicken may change.*

- *To make it spicier, add some chilli flakes to the sauce.*

- *Plain flour can also work, but cornflour gives a crispier texture to the chicken.*

AIR FRY

- *Cook at 200°C for 18–20 minutes. Add the sauce ingredients to the pan as above and then coat the chicken.*

TOMATO MUSHROOM PASTA

Using a base of onion, tomatoes and mushrooms creates a super simple dish that has a wonderful flavour balance, especially when cooked with garlic, paprika and chilli flakes. This sauce is thick, juicy and delicious, and all made in one pan. You can then add your cooked pasta and stir it through for a wonderful pasta dish that's ready in about 20 minutes. I add spinach at the end and simply stir it through, but just leave it out if you aren't a fan. I use any mushrooms that I happen to have in the fridge, but chestnut mushrooms are my favourite because of the flavour they bring.

SERVES: 4+

PREP: 5 minutes
COOK: 15 minutes
LASTS: Best served fresh

500g pasta of choice
1 tbsp olive oil
1 red onion, sliced
400g cherry tomatoes, halved
400g mushrooms, sliced
2–3 garlic cloves, crushed
1 tsp smoked paprika
½ tsp chilli flakes
50–75g fresh spinach
Salt and pepper

Fill a large pan with water and bring to the boil. Salt the water and pour in the pasta.

Cook the pasta for 1–2 minutes less than the packet instructions.

While the pasta is cooking, grab a large frying pan and set over a medium-high heat. Add the oil and fry the onion for 1–2 minutes until softened.

Add the tomatoes and mushrooms to the pan and cook for a few minutes until the tomatoes are softened and the mushrooms are cooked. Add the garlic, smoked paprika and chilli flakes and stir to combine. The mixture should have softened and created its own sauce. Add the spinach and stir through.

Pour the cooked pasta into the pan, or vice versa, and combine. Season with salt and pepper and serve immediately.

NOTES

• I like to use chestnut mushrooms, but any will work well.

15-MINUTE CARBONARA

I have made this carbonara endless times because it really is ready in 15 minutes and it's so rich and flavourful. It's perfect for you and a partner or friend as it serves two, however, you can easily multiply the quantities for more, although you might need a bigger pan! I tend to use just egg yolks as they give a more classic flavour, but you can use one egg instead of two yolks for each person you are serving. I use bacon lardons as they are easier to find in the supermarket, but if you can get guanciale you should definitely try it, it's the elite.

SERVES: 2

PREP: 2 minutes
COOK: 12–15 minutes
LASTS: Best served fresh

150g spaghetti
Splash of olive oil
2–3 rashers of bacon or 200g
  bacon lardons
4 egg yolks
35g Parmesan, grated
Pepper

Fill a large saucepan with water. Salt the water and bring to the boil. Once boiling, add the spaghetti and cook according to the packet instructions.

While the pasta is cooking, heat the olive oil in a saucepan. Add the bacon and cook until crispy.

While the bacon is cooking, add the egg yolks, Parmesan and pepper to a bowl and whisk to combine.

Once the bacon is crispy, turn off the heat and leave it in the pan.

Drain the cooked pasta, reserving some of the pasta cooking water in a mug, then transfer the pasta to the bacon pan. Pour in the egg and cheese mixture while still off the heat and add 1–2 tablespoons of the pasta cooking water. Stir to combine – the sauce should come together, thicken and be glossy. Divide between your bowls and enjoy.

NOTES

- You can use pancetta, or the classic guanciale, instead of bacon rashers or lardons.

- If you don't have Parmesan, you can use pecorino or Parmigiano Reggiano.

- Use 1 egg per 2 egg yolks if you want a slightly lighter dish, and if you don't have a way of using up the egg whites.

30

BAKED GNOCCHI

Gnocchi is something you can make yourself, but for ease, everyday shop-bought is totally fine. The tomato sauce for this beauty is made up of simple ingredients but it's full of flavour, so by the time you stir through the gnocchi, pour it into your dish and top with mozzarella, you've got a heart-warming one-pan dish that is a total crowd-pleaser. It's a beautiful vegetarian dish, but you could add meat if you want. I serve my Dough Balls from page 236 on the side for one of my favourite combos.

SERVES: 4–6

PREP: 20 minutes
COOK: 35 minutes
LASTS: Best served fresh

1–2 tbsp olive oil
1 medium onion, finely chopped
2–3 garlic cloves, chopped
Salt and pepper
1 tsp dried Italian herbs
800g tinned chopped tomatoes
500g fresh gnocchi
150g mozzarella, grated
Fresh basil leaves, to serve

Preheat the oven to 200°C/180°C fan and grab a large baking dish.

Add the olive oil to a large pan and set over a medium heat. Add the finely chopped onion and begin to sweat and soften. Add the garlic and fry for 1–2 minutes. Add some salt and pepper and the dried Italian herbs and mix in.

Pour in the chopped tomatoes and cook for a couple of minutes to incorporate. Pour the gnocchi into the pan and coat in the sauce. Pour into the baking dish. Sprinkle the mozzarella over the top.

Bake in the oven for 20–25 minutes until the cheese has melted and turned golden. Sprinkle on some basil leaves and serve.

NOTES

- *For a bit of heat, add 1–2 teaspoons of chilli flakes to the sauce.*

- *Swap the mozzarella for Cheddar cheese instead if you prefer.*

- *You can use any type of short pasta instead of gnocchi for a simple tomato pasta bake. It just needs to be cooked for 2 minutes less than the packet instructions before adding to the sauce.*

OVEN-BAKED RISOTTO

People can be put off making risotto because they think you have to stand there for ages and slave over the stove, but you really don't. This super-easy recipe is much more of a one-pot style where you put it all into one casserole dish, then bake in the oven for an effortless dinner. It's a brilliant way to use up leftovers and I tend to use whatever meat I have cooked during the week, as well as some frozen veg, which most people always have in the freezer ready to go. I use white wine, but you can swap this for more stock if you prefer. Stir the risotto slightly throughout the cooking if you're worried it might stick to your pot.

SERVES: 4+

PREP: 20 minutes
COOK: 25 minutes
LASTS: Best served fresh

35g unsalted butter

1 medium onion, finely chopped

200g leftover cooked meat, such as bacon or chicken

300g risotto rice

125ml white wine

750ml chicken or vegetable stock

100g frozen peas

65g Parmesan, grated

Preheat the oven to 200°C/180°C fan and grab an ovenproof dish.

Place the ovenproof dish over the hob on a medium-high heat, then add the butter to melt and cook the onion until softened. Add the leftover cooked meat to the pan and cook into the onion.

Add the risotto rice and cook for a further few minutes, stirring well, until mixed.

Pour in the wine and let it cook out for a minute or two. Pour in the stock and peas. Cover the top of the dish with a lid and place in the oven.

Cook the risotto in the oven for 20 minutes, stirring every 5–10 minutes to prevent the bottom catching.

Once cooked, remove from the oven, stir through the Parmesan and serve immediately.

NOTES

- You can use any leftover meat you have, or even fry off some meat first to use in the dish.

- If you don't have peas, you can use other frozen veg, or add them as well as the peas. The wine does cook out, but you can use more stock instead if you want the dish to be alcohol-free.

SLOW COOKER

- To make in a slow cooker, fry off the onion in the slow-cooker pot or in a pan. Add all the ingredients, except the Parmesan, to the slow cooker, then cook on low for 2 hours, stirring occasionally. Stir through the Parmesan and serve.

VEGGIE CHILLI

I will admit that I never thought so many of you would want my veggie chilli recipe. It's such a classic and basic dish, but I guess everyone does it differently. I prefer making a veggie chilli to a meat chilli because it makes a nice change and you can pack in SO much flavour. A base mixture of onion, carrot and celery, plus peppers, chopped tomatoes, kidney beans, cannellini beans and stock creates a wonderfully rich and delicious chilli that everyone will adore. It's so easy, an all-in-one pot and a classic dish for any night of the week.

SERVES: 6+

PREP: 10 minutes
COOK: 35–40 minutes
LASTS: Best served fresh

2–3 tbsp olive oil
2 medium onions, chopped
2 medium carrots, finely chopped
2 celery sticks, finely chopped
1 red pepper, chopped
1 green pepper, chopped
4 garlic cloves, finely chopped
1–2 tbsp tomato purée
400g tin chopped tomatoes
400g tin kidney beans, drained
400g tin cannellini beans, drained
400ml vegetable stock
25g dark chocolate
Salt and pepper

Spices

2 tbsp chilli powder
1 tsp ground cumin
1 tsp smoked paprika
1 tsp chilli flakes
1 tsp dried oregano
1 tsp dried mixed herbs
2–3 bay leaves
½ tsp dried coriander

Pour the olive oil into a large pan over a medium-high heat. Add the finely chopped onion, carrots and celery and fry for a few minutes until softened. Add the peppers and cook for a couple of minutes. Add the garlic, tomato purée and all of the spices and cook for a further couple of minutes.

Pour in the chopped tomatoes, kidney beans, cannellini beans and vegetable stock and stir through. Finally, add the dark chocolate, season with salt and pepper and simmer for 25–30 minutes until thickened, cooked through and delicious.

NOTES

- I serve my chilli with rice, tortilla chips and some guacamole.

- You can adapt the spices however you please. For a hot kick, add some fresh chilli.

SLOW COOKER

- To make in a slow cooker, add all the ingredients to the slow cooker and cook on high for 3½–4 hours or low for 7–8 hours. Once cooked, stir through 1 tablespoon of cornflour dissolved in 1 tablespoon of cold water.

CHICKPEA AND SPINACH CURRY

Who doesn't want to enjoy a curry ready in less than 30 minutes? Whack it all into a pan and cook together to make a thick and creamy curry with SO much flavour. I fry off my onion and garlic and add all the spices to create a ton of zing, but adding the tomato, chickpeas, stock and coconut milk takes it up another level. I include spinach for nutrition and colour, and because I adore it with the chickpeas. Serve this with rice and you have a glorious dinner ready very quickly. It also freezes super well for meal prepping and is fantastic in a slow cooker too.

SERVES: 4+

PREP: 20 minutes
COOK: 20–30 minutes
LASTS: Best served fresh

2 tbsp olive oil
1 medium onion, finely chopped
3 garlic cloves, finely chopped
1½ tsp smoked paprika
1 tsp cayenne pepper
1 tsp ground coriander
Pinch of chilli flakes
2 tbsp tomato purée
800g tinned chickpeas, drained
250ml vegetable stock
400ml tin coconut milk
1 tbsp cornflour dissolved in water
200g spinach

Heat the olive oil in a large pan over a medium-high heat and add the finely chopped onion. Fry for a few minutes to soften. Add the garlic, smoked paprika, cayenne pepper, ground coriander, chilli flakes and tomato purée and cook for a few more minutes.

Add the drained chickpeas, vegetable stock and coconut milk and stir to combine. Simmer for 15–20 minutes until the chickpeas are cooked.

Add the dissolved cornflour and stir through, then add the spinach. Stir to combine and simmer for a further couple of minutes. Serve immediately.

NOTES

- *I serve my curry with coriander, rice and naan for a delicious dinner.*

- *You can substitute one of the tins of chickpeas for lentils.*

SLOW COOKER

- *To make in a slow cooker, add all the ingredients, except the cornflour and spinach, to the slow cooker and cook on high for 3½–4 hours or low for 7–8 hours. Once cooked, stir through the cornflour and spinach to thicken and serve.*

30

ROASTED RED PEPPER SOUP

I love soup. Some people may call me boring because of this, but I adore it. I don't get bored as there are so many flavours and ideas, but this roasted red pepper soup is my ultimate favourite. Simply roast red peppers in the oven until softened (or buy them pre-roasted from the shop), then add all the ingredients to a blender and YOU HAVE SOUP. This makes a decent amount as I prefer to produce a bigger batch and then freeze it all in portions. Serve with bread, as it is, or dunk an entire sandwich in it... I don't judge.

SERVES: 4–6+

PREP: 20 minutes
COOK: 50 minutes
LASTS: 2–3 days,
in the fridge

6 red peppers
Drizzle of olive oil
Salt and pepper
1 medium onion, chopped
3–4 garlic cloves, finely chopped
100g sun-dried tomatoes
700ml vegetable stock

Preheat the oven to 220°C/200°C fan and grab a large baking tray.

Cut the peppers into chunks and place onto the tray. Drizzle with oil and season with salt and pepper. Roast in the oven for 35–40 minutes.

When the peppers are towards the end of their roasting, add the onion and garlic to a pan with a drizzle of olive oil and cook until translucent.

Add the roasted peppers, cooked onion and garlic, sun-dried tomatoes and vegetable stock to a blender and blend until smooth. Pour back into the pan if it needs reheating and enjoy.

NOTES

- If you want to save time, use jarred roasted peppers – you'll need about 500g peppers.

- To make it spicier, add 1–2 teaspoons of chilli flakes when you are frying off the onion and garlic.

- You can make this ahead and freeze portions.

SLOW COOKER

- To make in a slow cooker, add all the ingredients to the slow cooker and cook on high for 3–4 hours, or low for 7–8 hours. Once cooked, blitz until smooth.

FRITTATA

I feel like a frittata is always overlooked and passed over for the classic omelette, but I really do love a frittata. It's so simple and easy to make and has a great easy-dinner vibe. You can adapt it to suit whatever you have left over in your fridge, as well as theming it to what you want. For example, I use a mixture of bacon lardons, asparagus and feta in this frittata, but you do you! This recipe is more of a guide so you know quantities and timings, but add what you wish. Other flavour combinations that I love are spinach and pepper, and ham and mushroom. It's entirely up to you!

SERVES: 4

PREP: 20 minutes
COOK: 20–30 minutes
LASTS: Best served fresh

150g bacon lardons
150g asparagus spears, chopped
   into 2.5cm (1in) pieces
8 eggs
65ml whole milk
1–2 garlic cloves, finely chopped
Salt and pepper
150g feta cheese, chopped

Preheat the oven to 200°C/180°C fan.

In a medium ovenproof frying pan, fry the bacon lardons and asparagus spears until the bacon is cooked and crispy.

While the bacon and asparagus are frying, add the eggs, milk, garlic and some salt and pepper to a bowl and mix to combine. Pour this over the bacon and asparagus off the heat and sprinkle over the chunks of feta.

Bake in the oven for 15–20 minutes until golden.

NOTES

- *You can use any vegetables and/or meat you fancy, or whatever you have in your fridge, just make sure you pre-cook them in the pan first before baking.*

- *You can sprinkle the finished dish with chopped spring onions, if you like.*

FRYING PAN PIZZAS

Pizza is my dream of dreams, but I like to make certain dishes as easy as possible. Yes, you do need to make the dough and let that sit for a certain amount of time, but it's worth it. Prep the sauce while the dough is resting, as well as the rest of the toppings. Lightly flour a surface to roll out the dough, then add to a pan. The combination of cooking over the hob while finishing under the grill works wonders as it perfectly cooks the dough and melts the cheese.

SERVES: 2

PREP: 60 minutes
PROVE: 30 minutes
COOK: 10 minutes
LASTS: Best served fresh

400g plain flour, plus extra for dusting
7g dried active yeast
2 tbsp olive oil
250–275ml water
Pinch of salt

Toppings

400g tin chopped tomatoes
1 tsp chilli flakes
1 tsp dried oregano
1 tsp garlic powder
1 tsp onion powder
2 tbsp olive oil
50–100g mozzarella, grated

Other Toppings (optional)

Roasted veggies
Cooked sausages
Pepperoni
Ham
Cooked chicken

Add the flour, yeast, oil and 200ml of the water to a bowl with the salt and bring together with a spatula. Gradually add the rest of the water if needed until you have a slightly sticky dough. Tip this onto a floured surface and knead for 10 minutes until the dough is smooth and soft and no longer sticky. Place the dough in a lightly oiled bowl, cover with clingfilm and leave to rest for 30 minutes.

Toppings

While the dough is resting, add the chopped tomatoes to a bowl with the chilli flakes, dried oregano, garlic powder and onion powder and stir to combine. Prepare your other toppings if required.

Split the dough into 2 pieces and roll each one into a circle about 23–25cm (9–10in) in diameter.

Heat a large ovenproof frying pan over a high heat and add 1 tablespoon of oil. Place one of the circles of dough into the heated pan, then spoon over half of the tomato mixture.

Sprinkle on the cheese, any other toppings you are using and fry for 1–2 minutes until the bottom is golden.

Transfer the pan to your grill and grill for 2–3 minutes until the top is cooked, the cheese is melted and it looks delicious. Repeat with the second piece of dough and remaining toppings.

NOTES

- Flavour the pizza sauce however you fancy, I just like these particular spices.

- If you want a cheesier topping, swap the mozzarella for a stronger cheese such as Cheddar.

Savoury Snacks & Sides

CHEESE AND BACON MUFFINS

I have always loved the combination of cheese and bacon and this super basic recipe is quick to make, plus the muffins are amazing when warm and fresh out of the oven. I love using mature Cheddar cheese, but you can use mild Cheddar, extra mature, or even Red Leicester. Make these quickly in a bowl with a spatula, you definitely don't need a mixer! They also freeze really well for when you need a savoury snack or side.

MAKES: 12

PREP: 10 minutes
BAKE: 20–22 minutes
COOL: 15 minutes
LASTS: 2+ days,
at room temperature

300g self-raising flour
100g mature Cheddar cheese,
    grated, plus extra for sprinkling
80ml sunflower oil
250ml whole milk
1 egg
200g cooked bacon lardons
Salt and pepper

Preheat the oven to 200°C/180°C fan and line a 12-hole muffin tray with tulip muffin cases.

In a large bowl, mix the flour, cheese, oil, milk, egg, bacon and seasoning with a spatula as little as possible until combined. Season with salt and pepper. Divide the mixture between the 12 cases and sprinkle on some extra cheese.

Bake for 20–22 minutes until golden. Leave to cool for 15 minutes before enjoying warm or leave to cool fully.

NOTES

- *You can use smoked or unsmoked bacon, whichever you prefer. You can also switch the bacon to ham.*

- *To make these veggie, switch the lardons for cooked onions.*

FETA GARLIC MUFFINS

Savoury muffins are one of my faaaavourite bakes because they're an easy one-bowl recipe – all you need to do is shove the ingredients in a bowl and mix. The mixture of feta, with a ton of garlic, a hint of Parmesan and some spinach is a wonderful flavour combination in a super-light muffin. The milk and oil create the lovely light batter – so make sure not to overmix! Within the hour you can have wonderfully warm and heavenly muffins.

MAKES: 12

PREP: 10 minutes
BAKE: 25–30 minutes
COOL: 10 minutes
LASTS: 2+ days,
at room temperature

350g self-raising flour
300ml whole milk
75ml vegetable oil
1 egg
65g Parmesan, grated
175g feta cheese, crumbled
2 garlic cloves, finely chopped
75g spinach, chopped

Preheat the oven to 200°C/180°C fan and line a 12-hole muffin tray with tulip muffin cases.

Add the flour to a large mixing bowl, then add the milk, oil and egg. Mix briefly to start to combine. Add the Parmesan, feta, garlic and spinach and fold together.

Divide the mixture between the 12 cases. Bake in the oven for 25–30 minutes until golden and leave to cool for 10 minutes before enjoying.

NOTES

- *Leave out the spinach if you prefer, but it does add greenery and a nice flavour.*

- *For extra flavour, season with salt and pepper, but the feta and Parmesan are already quite salty.*

DOUGH BALLS

We all know dough balls, right? The ones that you dip into a garlic butter. Well, this is an incredibly simple six-ingredient version that is SO straightforward and much easier than you may think. The bread itself is a cheat's bread, made up of just three ingredients: self-raising flour, Greek yoghurt and baking powder. The baking powder is optional, but it makes the bread just a smidge lighter. While the bread bakes, you can make the garlic butter which also uses just three ingredients. I will happily sit and devour all of these, but they serve two people for an easy smaller-batch bake.

SERVES: 2

PREP: 10 minutes
BAKE: 20–25 minutes
LASTS: Best served fresh

250ml Greek yoghurt
250g self-raising flour, plus extra
   for dusting
½ tsp baking powder

Garlic Butter

4 garlic cloves, finely chopped
5–10g flat-leaf parsley, finely
   chopped
75g salted butter, at room
   temperature

Preheat the oven to 200°C/180°C fan and grab a baking tray.

Add the yoghurt, flour and baking powder to the bowl of a mixer fitted with the dough hook attachment. Mix for 5–7 minutes. If you don't have a mixer, mix together with a spatula in a bowl for at least 7 minutes until the dough comes together. Tip the dough onto a lightly floured work surface, as it will be sticky, and split into 12 pieces. You may need to cover your hands in flour to make this easier.

Roll into 12 balls. Place onto the baking tray and bake in the oven for 20–25 minutes until golden.

While they are baking, mix the garlic, parsley and butter together in a small bowl. Serve the garlic butter alongside the warm dough balls, ready for dunking.

NOTES

- *You can make the butter more or less garlicky depending on how you like it.*

- *Leave out the parsley if you prefer.*

AIR FRY

- *Cook at 180°C for 10–15 minutes, turning every few minutes to cook evenly.*

GARLIC ROASTED TOMATO FLATBREADS

For this recipe, you can make your own quick flatbreads with the same style of dough as the Dough Balls on page 196, or you can use shop-bought, I won't judge. Roasting the tomatoes with garlic, a drizzle of olive oil, salt, pepper and herbs while prepping the bread is easy, and it makes the tomatoes so full of flavour. I mix the rocket through the roasted tomatoes and pile them onto the flatbreads with the mozzarella, then bake until melted and gooey. Add a little drizzle of balsamic and you have one of my favourite lunchtime treats for two. You can adapt and change them if you prefer to top with grated Cheddar, or even add some roasted veggies.

SERVES: 2

PREP: 20 minutes
BAKE: 40 minutes
LASTS: Best served fresh

250ml Greek yoghurt
250g self-raising flour
½ tsp baking powder

Topping
250g cherry tomatoes, halved
4–5 garlic cloves, finely chopped
2 tbsp olive oil
1 tsp dried Italian herbs
Salt and pepper
50g rocket
100g mozzarella balls
Balsamic glaze

Preheat the oven to 200°C/180°C fan and grab a baking tray.

Topping

Add the tomatoes, garlic, olive oil, Italian herbs and some salt and pepper to the tray and mix well. Bake in the oven for 20–25 minutes until the tomatoes are roasted and softened.

Meanwhile, add the yoghurt, flour and baking powder to the bowl of a mixer fitted with the dough hook attachment. Mix for 5–7 minutes. Tip the dough onto a lightly floured work surface, as it will be sticky, and split the mixture in half. Lightly press into two flatbreads about 5mm (¼in) thick.

Place the flatbreads onto a large baking tray and bake in the oven for 10–15 minutes while the tomatoes are roasting.

Once the tomatoes have roasted, mix through the rocket. Divide the mixture between the two cooked flatbreads. Top with the mozzarella cheese.

Return your flatbreads to the oven for another 5–10 minutes for the cheese to melt. Once cooked, drizzle with balsamic glaze and enjoy.

NOTES

- *If you want to save time, use two shop-bought flatbreads.*

- *If you don't have cherry tomatoes, you can use larger tomatoes, just quarter them before roasting.*

- *You can use grated mozzarella instead of mozzarella balls if you prefer.*

CRUSTY BREAD

I have adored baking for most of my life, but everyone always thinks about sweet recipes when they think of baking. However, I love baking homemade bread as well because it's so therapeutic, it's so fresh and it's so simple to make. Plus, this easy recipe uses only five ingredients, it doesn't require kneading and it creates a beautifully textured bread that is the perfect accompaniment to lots and lots of dishes in this book. I use it to dunk into my Roasted Red Pepper Soup on page 220 and for dipping into my Baked Feta and Tomato Dip on page 244. If you don't eat it all on the day, slice and freeze and then you can toast a slice whenever you need!

SERVES: 4+

PREP: 20 minutes
PROVE: 2+ hours
BAKE: 45 minutes
COOL: 15 minutes
LASTS: Best served fresh

500g bread flour, plus extra
  for dusting
10g dried active yeast
1 tsp salt
1 tsp caster sugar
350ml warm water

Add the bread flour, yeast, salt and sugar to a large bowl. Mix together briefly and then pour in the warm water. Mix together with a spatula until it comes together to form a wet dough. Cover the bowl with clingfilm and leave in a warm place for at least 2 hours, or until it has doubled in size.

Towards the end of the rising, preheat the oven to 220°C/200°C fan and grab a cast-iron pot and place it in the oven to preheat as well.

Turn the dough onto a lightly floured surface and bring together to form a ball as best as you can. The dough will still be very sticky, so I use a dough scraper or spatula to do this.

Transfer the dough to a larger piece of parchment paper. Remove the cast-iron pot from the oven, place the dough on its parchment paper into the pot, add the lid and bake for 30 minutes. After 30 minutes, remove the lid and bake for another 15 minutes.

Cool for at least 15 minutes before removing the bread from the pot and serving.

NOTES

- *If you don't have a cast iron pot, you can use a preheated high-sided pot or roasting pan with a lid.*

HOMEMADE HOUMOUS

When I say I am obsessed with houmous (or hummus), I am not joking. I used to say I hated it, but I had never actually tried it… I know, the worst. However, while discovering how much I adore all things mezze, I realised houmous is by far my favourite dish. This simple recipe for homemade houmous is ready in just 15 minutes. You can freeze portions if there are only a few eating it, or you can serve the entire batch at a party – it's so good for dipping other goodies into, as well, like my homemade Tortilla Chips on page 247.

SERVES: 4–6

PREP: 15 minutes
LASTS: 2+ days,
in the fridge (but
best served fresh)

400g tin chickpeas, drained and
   liquid reserved
50ml lemon juice
50g tahini
1–2 garlic cloves, finely chopped
Salt and pepper
30–40ml olive oil
30–50ml chickpea water

Topping
Olive oil
Paprika
Sumac

Add the chickpeas, lemon juice, tahini, garlic, salt and pepper to a blender. Add 30ml of the oil and 30ml of the chickpea water and begin to blend. Add more olive oil and/or chickpea water if you need to create a smoother texture.

Once blended, pour into a bowl and drizzle with a little olive oil and sprinkle over some paprika and sumac if desired.

NOTES

- *To make this houmous sweet-chilli-flavoured, add 1–2 tablespoons of sweet chilli sauce while blending, replacing some of the oil/chickpea water.*

- *To make it red-pepper-flavoured, add 150g jarred, roasted red peppers to the blender and omit the oil.*

- *I sometimes split the portion and freeze half for a later date. Defrost in the fridge the day before you want it.*

BAKED FETA AND TOMATO DIP

If you're on a video-based social media platform, you may recognise the idea of a baked feta and tomato pasta dish. I have made this myself a fair few times as it's really easy, but then I started changing it up a little and not even adding the pasta. That gives you this rich and creamy dip that's perfect to slather on homemade bread, dip vegetables in, or add to the side of a dish such as jacket potatoes. I love the tomatoes, shallot and pepper mixed in with the flavours of the garlic, chilli flakes and of course... the feta.

SERVES: 3–4

PREP: 10 minutes
BAKE: 20–25 minutes
LASTS: 1–2 days in the fridge (but best served fresh)

500g cherry tomatoes, halved
1 red pepper, thinly sliced
At least 4 garlic cloves, thinly sliced
1 large shallot or 1 red onion, thinly sliced
1–2 tsp chilli flakes
Salt and pepper
Olive oil, for drizzling
200g feta
Handful of fresh basil, chopped

Preheat the oven to 200°C/180°C fan and grab a medium baking dish.

Stir all the ingredients, except the feta and basil, together in a bowl and pour into the baking dish. Place the feta in the middle. Bake in the oven for 20–25 minutes.

Sprinkle over the fresh basil. Dunk freshly baked Crusty Bread from page 240.

NOTES

- If you don't have cherry tomatoes, you can use larger tomatoes chopped into quarters.

- If you want it spicier, add freshly sliced chilli instead of the chilli flakes.

- You can serve this with a small handful of chopped fresh basil, if you like.

30

HOMEMADE CHEESE DIP AND TORTILLA CHIPS

This luxurious cheese dip, with homemade crunchy tortilla chips, is ready in under 30 minutes. The tortilla chips are wraps that you can slice up into a chip size, baked with a little oil while you make the incredibly easy dip. Add all of the cheese dip ingredients into a pan, melt over a low heat until smooth, cheesy and GOOD. I use the mustard and paprika to combat the sweetness of the evaporated milk, alongside a mature Cheddar cheese of dreams. If you want to use a milder or stronger cheese, you can, of course. Adapt the recipe to whatever you prefer, as this is a great small batch dip for movie night, a starter, or just because you want cheese.

SERVES: 2–4

PREP: 10 minutes
BAKE: 10 minutes
LASTS: Best served fresh

Tortilla Chips

2–3 tortilla wraps
Olive oil spray

Cheese Dip

150g mature Cheddar cheese
150ml evaporated milk
1 tbsp cornflour
½ tsp mustard powder
½ tsp paprika
Pinch of salt and pepper

Preheat the oven to 200°C/180°C fan and grab a large baking tray.

Tortilla Chips

Chop the tortillas into small triangles and spritz with oil. Bake in the oven for 7–10 minutes, turning halfway, until crunchy.

Cheese Dip

While the tortillas are baking, add the cheese, evaporated milk, cornflour, mustard powder, paprika, salt and pepper to a pan and melt over a medium heat until smooth.

Dunk the freshly baked tortilla chips into the cheese dip and enjoy.

NOTES

- *If you want to save time, you can use shop-bought tortilla chips.*

- *You can use any strength of Cheddar cheese you want, depending on what you prefer.*

- *Leave out the mustard and paprika if you prefer.*

GARLIC MUSHROOMS

I'm always after a quick dish that I can serve on the side, at a lunch or when having a dinner party as part of a food platter, and these garlic mushrooms are always so popular. Five ingredients create a super-easy dish packed full of flavour. I love using chestnut button mushrooms because they're so tasty, but you can use a mixture of other mushrooms, or even swap the mushrooms for bite-sized pieces of chicken.

SERVES: 2–3

PREP: 5 minutes
COOK: 10–15 minutes
LASTS: 2+ days,
in the fridge (but
best served fresh)

500g chestnut button mushrooms
25g salted butter
3 garlic cloves, finely chopped
Pinch of pepper
1 handful of flat-leaf parsley,
   roughly chopped

Preheat the oven to 200°C/180°C fan and grab a small baking dish.

Add the mushrooms, butter, garlic and pepper to the dish. Bake in the oven for 10–15 minutes until the mushrooms are the texture you prefer. Stir through the parsley and enjoy.

NOTES

- *Serve with my Crusty Bread on page 240 for a delicious snack.*

- *You can use white mushrooms, or any others, just chop to a small size.*

- *If you don't have fresh parsley, 1 teaspoon of dried parsley also works well.*

HALLOUMI BACON BITES

Why would you not combine two of the best ingredients in the world?! I question how I haven't shared this recipe before because it's such an incredible combination of salty bacon, tasty halloumi and a sticky chilli honey glaze. With only five ingredients, it's SO easy to make. Great as a snack, a side dish, something for an occasion, or even take it up a level and wrap the bites in puff pastry to make a delicious treat (like a sausage roll). You can use smoked or unsmoked bacon, plain or chilli halloumi... anything you fancy.

SERVES: 2–3

PREP: 10 minutes
BAKE: 20–25 minutes
LASTS: Best served fresh

250g halloumi
4 rashers of bacon, halved
50g clear honey
Chilli flakes
Pepper

Preheat the oven to 200°C/180°C fan and grab a baking tray.

Cut the halloumi into 8 pieces and then wrap each one with a bacon rasher. Place onto the baking tray and bake in the oven for 20–25 minutes until golden and the bacon is cooked. Turn halfway through for more even cooking.

Towards the end of cooking, mix the honey, some chilli flakes and pepper in a small bowl. Drizzle over the cooked halloumi bacon bites or use it as a dip.

NOTES

- *Bacon rashers are recommended as they are the correct width, but you can slice a piece of back bacon in half to make it the right size.*

- *If you're serving more than 3 people, the quantities can easily be multiplied.*

AIR FRY

- *Cook at 190°C for 10–12 minutes, turning halfway through.*

5

TACO CUPS

Tacos are one of my favourite dishes and I just don't get bored of them. They are a fun way to eat food, especially if you make them at the table and top them with whatever you like. However, they are a smidge faffy, so taco cups are my alternative to make them easier to prep, bake and serve. This recipe uses half a mini tortilla wrap per cup, filled with a simple homemade beef and tomato filling full of spice, scattered with cheese. I make these so that the cheese melts and goes golden, and topping them with a little bit of crunchy lettuce and a dollop of dip gives perfection in every bite.

MAKES: 12

PREP: 10 minutes
BAKE: 15–20 minutes
LASTS: Best served fresh

6 mini tortillas
1 tbsp olive oil
1 white onion, chopped
250g beef mince
1 tsp chilli powder
1 tsp smoked paprika
1 tsp garlic powder
1 tsp onion powder
1 tsp chilli flakes
1 tsp dried oregano
Salt and pepper
200g tinned chopped tomatoes
200g Cheddar cheese or
  mozzarella, grated
100g lettuce, chopped
Guacamole or tomato salsa

Preheat the oven to 200°C/180°C fan and grab a 12-hole muffin tray.

Cut the mini tortillas in half, then make 12 cups by folding them into the holes in the muffin tray.

Set a frying pan over a medium-high heat and drizzle in the oil. Fry the onion until softened, then add the beef mince and fry until browned. Add the chilli powder, smoked paprika, garlic powder, onion powder, chilli flakes, oregano and some salt and pepper. Fry for a minute, then add the chopped tomatoes and stir through.

Divide the mixture between the 12 taco cups, then top with the grated cheese. Bake in the oven for 15–20 minutes until the cheese is melted and golden brown. Top with the chopped lettuce and a dollop of guacamole or tomato salsa and serve.

NOTES

- *If you don't have tinned tomatoes, you can use chopped fresh cherry tomatoes instead.*

- *Adapt the spices to whatever you prefer.*

AIR FRY

- *Cook at 200°C for 5–7 minutes.*

PIZZA QUESADILLA

Pizza is one of the best foods, so why not give it a fun little twist to make the perfect snack for a couple of people, or for when you fancy something a little different and fun. I love making pizza, such as my Frying Pan Pizzas on page 226, but sometimes you need something quicker. In less than 30 minutes, you can have this heavenly, cheesy dish. Two large tortillas, smothered in an easy homemade pizza sauce, sandwiched with a load of cheese and your favourite pizza toppings. Fry it in a frying pan, flipping it every so often to make it melty, golden and YUMMY. This is a great recipe for two to share as a snack, but you can easily make it a meal with other side dishes like my Giant Stuffed Hasselback Potatoes (page 260) or Potato Salad (page 258). It's also equally good cold for lunch the next day!

SERVES: 2

PREP: 15 minutes
BAKE: 10 minutes
LASTS: Best served fresh

2 large tortilla wraps
75g mozzarella, grated
50g cooked meat of choice
15g Parmesan, grated

Sauce

2 tbsp tomato purée
½ tsp onion powder
½ tsp garlic powder
½ tsp Italian mixed herbs
½ tsp dried oregano or basil
½ tsp chilli flakes
Salt and pepper
2 tbsp water

Sauce

In a small bowl, mix all the sauce ingredients together.

Lay the tortillas out and spread over the sauce. Sprinkle one with the mozzarella, add the cooked meat and sprinkle over the Parmesan. Press on the second tortilla, sauce down, and then transfer the quesadilla to a large frying pan.

Heat over a medium-high heat for 2–3 minutes, then flip carefully and continue cooking. Continue to heat and flip until both sides are golden and the cheese has melted. Slice into segments and enjoy.

NOTES

- *To make this veggie, swap the meat for roasted veggies or some chopped veg and leave out the Parmesan.*

- *The spices are optional and changeable to your taste.*

30

BANG BANG CAULIFLOWER

Whenever I want something a little fun, such as an easy side dish that is full of flavour and I know is popular, I think of this. Tasty roasted cauliflower, coated in a spicy and delicious sauce and it's super easy to make. It may sound faffy, but honestly you just mix the cauliflower in the marinade, bread the pieces and roast. While it roasts, prep the sauce and then all you have to do is toss the roasted cauliflower through it. If you want to feed a crowd, simply multiply the quantities to cater for however many people you need to serve.

SERVES: 4+

PREP: 30 minutes
BAKE: 20–30 minutes
LASTS: Best served fresh

50g plain flour
50g cornflour
2 tsp paprika
125ml whole milk
1 tsp lemon juice
100g panko breadcrumbs
1 large cauliflower, broken
    into florets

Sauce

3 tbsp mayo
2 tbsp sriracha
2 tbsp sweet chilli sauce
2 tsp dark soy sauce
1 tbsp honey
1 tsp finely chopped garlic (or
    garlic paste)

To Serve

Sesame seeds
Sliced spring onions

Preheat the oven to 220°C/200°C fan and line a large baking tray with baking parchment.

Add the flour, cornflour and paprika to a bowl and stir. Add the milk and lemon juice and mix again. Add the breadcrumbs to a plate. Coat the cauliflower florets in the marinade and then coat in the breadcrumbs. Transfer to the lined baking tray. Roast in the oven for 20–30 minutes.

Sauce

Meanwhile, make the sauce by adding all the ingredients to a bowl and mixing together.

Once roasted, coat the cauliflower in the sauce. Top with sesame seeds and spring onions and enjoy.

NOTES

- *If you want this less spicy, remove the sriracha from the sauce.*

- *If you want a bit more heat, add some finely chopped chilli to the sauce.*

AIR FRY

- *Cook at 180°C for 20 minutes, shaking the cauliflower halfway through.*

POTATO SALAD

I feel like potato salad is underrated, but often shop-bought ones can be quite boring, so this recipe solves those problems. While you boil the potatoes, you can make the sauce. It may sound like a few ingredients, but honestly this mix of mayo and oil with finely chopped shallots, seasoning, mustard, vinegar and parsley takes just seconds to make. I run my potatoes under cold water once they have finished cooking, then stir everything together. You have to take the finished bowl away from me, though, because I want to devour ALL OF IT. It's so full of flavour and so good!

SERVES: 4–6

PREP: 10 minutes
COOK: 15–20 minutes
LASTS: 3 days,
in the fridge (but
best served fresh)

1kg new potatoes, chopped into
  2.5cm (1in) pieces
2–3 small shallots, finely chopped
Salt and pepper
100g mayonnaise
2–3 tbsp olive oil
1 small handful of flat-leaf parsley,
  chopped
½ tsp Dijon mustard
1 tsp white wine vinegar

Add the potatoes to a large pan and cover with boiling water. Boil in slightly salted water for 15–20 minutes until cooked.

In a large bowl, combine the shallots, some salt and pepper, the mayonnaise, olive oil, parsley, mustard and white wine vinegar.

Pour the potatoes into a colander and run under the cold tap to cool them down quickly. Leave to drain for a minute or two. Tip into the bowl with the rest of the ingredients and mix together.

NOTES

- *If you don't have new potatoes, you can use larger potatoes, just make sure to chop them small enough so that they cook in the same amount of time.*

30

GIANT STUFFED
HASSELBACK POTATOES

If you haven't ever had or seen anything hasselback before, it is one of my favourite things to do because you level up whatever you are serving tenfold. Using two wooden spoons along the sides of your large baking potatoes, you cut down at regular intervals but leave the bottom of the potato attached. Bake the potatoes in the oven until they're nice and crispy and this is where you go crazy: brush with garlic butter, put Cheddar cheese in each slice, then scatter with breadcrumbs and bake to melty perfection. You can stop there, but I then top mine with crispy bacon lardons, spring onions and my favourite dip. This recipe serves two, but you can multiply the quantities to serve more if you want.

SERVES: 2

PREP: 20 minutes
BAKE: 1+ hour
LASTS: Best served fresh

2 baking potatoes
Drizzle of olive oil
125g Cheddar cheese, sliced, plus
  extra (optional) grated, to serve
25g breadcrumbs, made from
  stale bread
100g bacon lardons, cooked
Dip of choice (optional)
Spring onions, sliced (optional)

Garlic butter

35g salted butter, melted
2 garlic cloves, crushed
1 small bunch of parsley, finely
  chopped

Preheat the oven to 220°C/200°C fan.

Place the handles of two wooden spoons on either side of the potatoes, then carefully slice at regular intervals until the knife meets the spoon handles to create the hasselback pattern. Rub lightly in olive oil and then bake in the oven for 1 hour.

In a small bowl, mix all the ingredients for the garlic butter together. At the end of the hour, remove the potatoes from the oven and brush over the garlic butter. Carefully insert slices of cheese in the gaps, then sprinkle over the breadcrumbs. Bake for a further 2–5 minutes until the cheese is melted.

Remove from the oven and transfer to a plate. Top with cooked bacon lardons and extra grated cheese, or with your favourite dip and some sliced spring onions, if you fancy.

NOTES

- *You can leave out the toppings if you prefer, or simply just scatter with extra grated cheese. You can use grated instead of sliced to fill the potatoes, but it's slightly messier.*

AIR FRY

- *Cook the potatoes at 200°C for 40–50 minutes, then insert the cheese slices and sprinkle with the breadcrumbs and cook for a further 2–3 minutes.*

Conversion Tables

Weights *

METRIC	IMPERIAL
15 g	½ oz
25 g	1 oz
40 g	1½ oz
50 g	2 oz
75 g	3 oz
100 g	4 oz
150 g	5 oz
175 g	6 oz
200 g	7 oz
225 g	8 oz
250 g	9 oz
275 g	10 oz
350 g	12 oz
375 g	13 oz
400 g	14 oz
425 g	15 oz
450 g	1 lb
550 g	1¼ lb
675 g	1½ lb
900 g	2 lb
1.5 kg	3 lb
1.75 kg	4 lb
2.25 kg	5 lb

*28.35g = 1oz but the measurements here have been rounded up or down to make conversion easier.

Volume

METRIC	IMPERIAL
25 ml	1 fl oz
50 ml	2 fl oz
85 ml	3 fl oz
150 ml	5 fl oz (¼ pint)
300 ml	10 fl oz (¼ pint)
450 ml	15 fl oz (¾ pint)
600 ml	1 pint
700 ml	1¼ pints
900 ml	1½ pints
1 litres	1¾ pints
1.2 litres	2 pints
1.25 litres	2¼ pints
1.5 litres	2½ pints
1.6 litres	2¾ pints
1.75 litres	3 pints
1.8 litres	3¼ pints
2 litres	3½ pints
2.1 litres	3¾ pints
2.25 litres	4 pints
2.75 litres	5 pints
3.4 litres	6 pints
3.9 litres	7 pints
5 litres	8 pints (1 gal)

Measurements

METRIC	IMPERIAL
0.5 cm	¼ inch
1 cm	½ inch
2.5 cm	1 inch
5 cm	2 inches
7.5 cm	3 inches
10 cm	4 inches
15 cm	6 inches
18 cm	7 inches
20 cm	8 inches
23 cm	9 inches
25 cm	10 inches
30 cm	12 inches

Oven Temperatures

140°C	275°F	Gas Mk 1
150°C	300°F	Gas Mk 2
165°C	325°F	Gas Mk 3
180°C	350°F	Gas Mk 4
190°C	375°F	Gas Mk 5
200°C	400°F	Gas Mk 6
220°C	425°F	Gas Mk 7
230°C	450°F	Gas Mk 8
240°C	475°F	Gas Mk 9

Index

Acknowledgements

I genuinely can't believe it's been ten years since Jane's Patisserie started, and the biggest thank you and acknowledgement I need to make is to you guys reading this. The people who have supported me since the beginning, and continue to support me with every adventure.

My followers and readers are the reason I am sat here writing this for my FOURTH book, and I still need to have a pinch me moment. For a girl who just loved baking and wanted to actually follow their passion, you guys made that possible.

My family has always supported me no matter what crazy idea I have yet. Whether it's pet sitting so I can go on a cake-ing adventure, helping me eat all the cake I make, or even just keep me sane when I feel like everything is becoming too much. Joan, Victor and Robert… you are the best (And Thor, Ralph and Max… of course)

Friends are the people who are there for you, no matter what. I am so lucky that my friends have supported me right from the beginning, and they continue to do so every single day. I often become anxious or nervous about my career and the Jane's Patisserie journey, but they back me every single time.

My Ebury team is full of people I can always trust to have the best ideas and support for my author journey, and now we are on book four?! It's utter madness. Thank you for letting me follow my dream with my books and do something I never thought was possible. Sam, Abby, Alice and Francesca… you are all THE BEST. I cannot thank you enough, yet again.

I continue to absolutely and utterly adore you Ellis, and I want everyone to know how brilliant you are. You see my vision with my recipes, and you know how to bring them to life every single time. Your style is amazing, and you STILL manage to get a decent photo of me, which I've always thought was impossible with shutting my eyes every time I smile.

Sarah and Alice, you guys are the brains behind the bakes in this book, and you make them all so perfectly. They look utterly scrumptious and delicious every time and your attention to detail is just perfection.

Thank you to every single person who believes in me and Jane's Patisserie, and bakes the recipes, and likes the photos on social media, and says hello in real life… you are kind, you are genuine, and you are the reason I get to do what I love. Thank you.

Jane x

Ebury Press an imprint of Ebury Publishing,
20 Vauxhall Bridge Road,
London SW1V 2SA

Ebury Press is part of the Penguin Random House group of companies
whose addresses can be found at global.penguinrandomhouse.com

Penguin
Random House
UK

First published by Ebury Press in 2024

www.penguin.co.uk

A CIP catalogue record for this book is available from the British Library

ISBN 9781529196856

Design: Studio Nic & Lou
Photography: Ellis Parrinder
Food Styling: Sarah Hardy
Prop Styling: Max Robinson

Printed and bound in Germany by Mohn Media Mohndruck GmbH

The authorised representative in the EEA is Penguin Random House Ireland,
Morrison Chambers, 32 Nassau Street, Dublin D02 YH68.